Rwitwika has b_____ can remember. As a p_____sisted of political leaders: members _____ Congress, MPs, MLAs and ministers. Hence, from a young age, she had the opportunity to study Indian politics. Her childhood interests soon turned into a passion as she pursued a degree in political science and economics from Wake Forest University. Eventually she completed a master's degree in Public Policy from Harvard and worked at the World Bank. But her passion for politics pulled her back in and she started a social enterprise, Swaniti Initiative, that supports elected officials (MPs and MLAs) on development issues. Now her work focuses on working with MPs on constituency-level matters. In 2014, she featured in the *Forbes* India's 30 under 30 list, she has been recognized by the White House as an Emerging Entrepreneur, by the British High Commission as a Young Leader, by the Australian Government as a Young Leader and by the World Economic Forum as a Young Global Leader, amongst other accolades. Politics continues to be her soft spot.

What Makes a Politician

RWITWIKA BHATTACHARYA-AGARWAL

HarperCollins *Publishers* India

First published in India in 2017 by
HarperCollins *Publishers* India

Copyright © Rwitwika Bhattacharya-Agarwal

P-ISBN: 978-93-5277-272-8
E-ISBN: 978-93-5277-273-5

2 4 6 8 10 9 7 5 3 1

Rwitwika Bhattacharya-Agarwal asserts the moral right
to be identified as the author of this work.

The views and opinions expressed in this book
are the author's own and the facts are as reported by her,
and the publishers are not in any way liable for the same.

All rights reserved. No part of this publication may be reproduced,
stored in a retrieval system, or transmitted, in any form or by any means,
electronic, mechanical, photocopying, recording or otherwise,
without the prior permission of the publishers.

HarperCollins *Publishers*
A-75, Sector 57, Noida, Uttar Pradesh 201301, India
1 London Bridge Street, London, SE1 9GF, United Kingdom
2 Bloor Street East, Toronto, Ontario M4W 1A8, Canada
Lvl 13, 201 Elizabeth Street (PO Box A565, NSW, 1235),
Sydney NSW 2000, Australia
195 Broadway, New York, NY 10007, USA

Typeset in 11/14 Bembo Std
by Jojy Philip, New Delhi

Printed and bound at
Thomson Press (India) Ltd

To my husband who has always believed in me.
To my Baba and Ma who are my pillar of support.
And to my Jethu and Mummum who have always been there

Contents

	Foreword	ix
1	Understanding the Book	1

Section I

2	What Is Politics?	17
3	What Is a Political Party?	38

Section II
Ensuring Professional Growth

4	How Do You Prepare for Politics Professionally?	67
5	How to Build Your Brand and Message?	89
6	How Do You Make Money When in Politics?	110

Section III
Preparing Emotionally for Politics

7	What Are the Personal Tolls of Politics?	135
8	What Is It Like to Be a Woman in Politics?	151
9	Closing Thoughts	164

Foreword

I have had the pleasure of working with the Swaniti Initiative to strengthen the healthcare infrastructure in my constituency, Kendrapara, through deployment of mobile health units. Rwitwika Bhattacharya, the author of this book, is also the founder of Swaniti. The existence of Swaniti, an organization that assists MPs in their constituency work, is a sign of the changing times and also, the reason for the need of this book.

The political scene is gradually evolving in our country. More politicians are equipping themselves with teams with the necessary domain knowledge. Simultaneously, there is now a growing ecosystem of people with skills from various backgrounds, especially younger citizens. Responsibilities are being delegated to people with expertise; transferable skill sets acquired by their prior experiences are being put to the best use in the political domain. There are various opportunities in the form of fellowships, consultancy, advisory and grassroots-level positions available for those who want to dip their toes in this field. There are more chances than ever before to rise on merit alone at the intersection of politics and policy. This is a new revolution of kinds – an actual democracy where there is space for everyone with the spirit of public service.

Now is an exciting time to be in the policy space with new,

improved organizational structures and systems materializing. This book speaks to the aspirations of those who aim to serve at the national level. It is a complete guide covering the very basics of our political system to building your brand, networking and even financially supporting yourself to help you on your journey. She has made a good attempt at defining the scope and nature of a parliamentarian's work and the various stakeholders she/he has to juggle with. The book is even more useful as a lot of our system is informal and closed in nature.

The result that is this book is built upon extensive research and cites many real-world examples. It has introspection exercises at the end of chapters providing for application of the knowledge, and it even points to other relevant resources for further reference. Rwitwika hasn't shied away from controversial topics like the prevalence of identity politics, lobbying or the fewer number of female politicians. Necessary emphasis has been given to the importance of intangible skills like charm, good communication and mobilization skills and the intangible costs like the effect on private life.

This book is a welcome move away from caricaturing, stereotyping or straightforward dismissing the work of public officials. The core sentiment of public service has been highlighted as a motivation. Anyone remotely interested in knowing or participating in the policy sphere should consider reading this.

Baijayant Panda
Member of the Lok Sabha

Chapter 1

Understanding the Book

Why the Book?

My tiny hands fit in the palm of my father's hand as he holds it lightly, taking me along to the red-bricked offices of ministers, high-ceilinged residences of parliamentarians, and congested party offices all over Delhi. My father is in the field of politics, and I have been following him around since I was ten years old. My parents believed in giving me exposure to as many things as possible. 'Only then will you know how the world works,' my mother would say with confidence. So I found myself encouraged to attend my father's meetings with high-powered politicians from a very young age. 'Make sure you also contribute a bit to the conversation,' my mother would say gently. In each meeting, I would find the confidence to ask a few questions.

When my father asked me to accompany him to meet with an upcoming Member of Parliament (MP) one lazy summer afternoon, I didn't think much of it. We headed to Ashoka Hotel, a standard meeting venue, sat down comfortably in the coffee shop that smelled like wet carpet in the middle of May. The young MP was on time and discussed politics and possibilities with my father over the next hour. As they began to wrap up their discussion, I remembered my mother's commandment and quickly asked him the only question I could think of:

'What got you interested in politics and how did you become an MP?'

I thought it was a simple question that would be interesting for him to answer; after all, he could see this as an opportunity to mentor a young girl of eleven. Instead, he frowned at me, looking as though I had said something preposterous. A long silence followed. He wiped that look off his face and replaced it with a patronising frown. He tilted his head back and after a slow sip of his coffee, answered: 'Why don't you grow up a bit, finish school, college and get a job and then we can speak again? You might be ready for an answer then.' He seemed satisfied with his answer and got up to leave. He saw nothing wrong with what he had said. However, I felt insulted and that exchange made a strong imprint on my memory.

I don't know if it was the arrogance of being a first time parliamentarian, the excitement of making it big at a young age, or disregard for a younger person, but he had felt it was appropriate to dismiss the question. The more I thought about the fundamental question of how one gets in to politics to emerge as an electoral representative nationally, the more intrigued I was. The young MP monopolized information on political success consciously. He belonged to an exclusive club of successful men and women who had made it in national electoral politics, and only they knew how to enter and rise up in politics.

After that meeting, I began to ask politicians I met while with my father about their entry into politics. The response was consistent in almost every scenario. Most Indian politicians I asked would quickly skim over the phase in their lives where they quit full-time jobs to pursue political passions and instead focus on that part of their careers after they had gotten in to politics. Their answers would be something like: 'I was pulled to public service and joined Party X. *Eventually*, I got a ticket and contested for an election. But after I won the election, I wanted to do more for my constituency.' The gap between deciding to join a party and running for office was captured with the word *'eventually'*.

This is true not only of parliamentarians and what they say; there is an equally large gap found in political biographies. Whether it is a biography of Prime Minister Narendra Modi or Narasimha Rao, little attention is devoted to the transition into politics; instead, there is disproportionately large discourse around their journeys after they enter in to politics. Having worked with American senators and elected representatives, I feel that Indian politics stands in sharp contrast to western democracy. For example, in the US, there is an established process of how talent is scouted, offered a ticket for respective parties, funded for candidacy and brought in to office.

In 2010, a classmate of mine from Florida decided to contest for the local representative's seat. He had served in the armed forces, worked for a top firm and graduated from a premier business school. He wanted to 'give back' to his community now. He went back to Florida and collected over a thousand signatures from people who endorsed his candidacy. He took this list to the head of the local Democratic Party and showed them proof of community support. The party took a few weeks to run a background check on him and gave him the clear to run for the primaries. As he was a particularly promising candidate, the party helped him raise money and connected him to the 'right' community leaders. He went on to win the primaries and the election seat at large. The party members had coached and supported him throughout the process. Such a well-formed structure does not seem to exist in India. Systems are informal and often mean that the most talented individuals do not end up pursuing politics.

In 2012, I founded the Swaniti Initiative, led by the desire to better understand politics. Swaniti is a non-profit that supports parliamentarians in constituency-based development issues. Conversations from my childhood with parliamentarians served to remind me of how dedicated politicians can be to constituency-level issues, and I saw this as an opportunity to engage political leaders in development discourse.

However, what has been even more fascinating is the kind of interest young professionals show in their desire to join the political sphere through organizations like Swaniti. We have received over five hundred applications from people from the best universities and professional firms for a small number of five job openings. A majority of these applicants see Swaniti as a way of finding exposure to the political life that they aspire toward. Following my colleagues' through their political journey, I have come to realize that while we have tremendous leadership potential in our country, the system is severely broken and needs nurturing.

Many of my colleagues have joined political parties, but there is no clear direction. They continue to be at the bottom rung of parties despite the hard work they put into understanding the system. They grapple with many questions: How do I match my talents with requirements in the party? How do I make myself useful as a party member? How do I leverage my contacts outside politics in the field?

The goal of this book is to answer these questions. As you consider entering politics as a profession, or if you are at the beginning of your political career, it is important to examine every element of the field. You must treat politics like any other profession: study it carefully and in great detail, connect with potential mentors, and build a strong network.

It is a particularly interesting time to be in politics; political winds are shifting and something phenomenal is happening in the space of governance.

Why Is This Book Important Now?

We live in a time of drastically changing political environments. The Arab Spring saw the youth of the Middle East coming out to the streets to question dictatorships; the Anna Hazare movement was a historic expression of discontent against corruption that brought down the Congress Party; most recently, Donald Trump's unexpected victory has shaken the American electoral establishment. There is global discontent with the status quo in politics and a desire for something new. Voters are taking this into their hands in order to find it.

A majority is rising up and taking charge. Political parties need to rethink their approach to politics and there is indication that several of them are already doing so. Leaders who are able to display their newer skill sets are gaining quick political capital and being pulled up the political ladder.

For example, my colleague from the World Bank quit his prospering career to join politics in 2012. He held degrees from top American universities and had offers of jobs with six-digit salaries from several private firms. However, he was determined to serve the public through politics. Without a family background in politics or social capital in the field, most people discouraged his 'rash' decision to move back to India to enter politics. But he was determined, articulate, and a great networker. In three short years, he found his way to the office of the chief minister. He convinced the chief minister of his allegiance to the party and that he wanted to add value.

The chief minister appreciated a young and educated man who was willing to help his government and gave him the responsibility of gathering ground-level data on development programmes. He had found his avenue and worked incredibly hard on the project. He delivered on the task he was assigned brilliantly. The chief minister found value in what he was doing and gave him additional responsibilities, each of which he delivered exceptionally well. He soon made it to the party's inner coterie. He has continued to work on election strategies, recruitment campaigns and media management, and is now vying for a ticket in the next election. The party has given him the temporary label of 'advisor' even as everybody expects a leadership position for him soon.

Other than individual instances, there is further evidence of systemic change for which we don't need to look far beyond Delhi. The Aam Aadmi Party (AAP) is one such party of professionals where people who have strong academic and work backgrounds have entered into politics. From Arvind Kejriwal who has had no background in governance beyond his years of activism on Right to Information, to star campaigners like Kumar Vishwas who was known much more so in the entertainment industry, to electoral candidates like Irom Sharmila, the party has consistently demonstrated a preference for bringing in people with stellar professional records, a keen interest in politics, but no political standing.

Two star AAP workers from the early days are Atishi Marlena, a Rhodes Scholar from Oxford University, and Roshan Shankar, a computer engineer from Stanford University. Both could have excelled in fields of their choosing but chose to enter political life. They rose swiftly within party ranks having demonstrated their value in the political process to the party leadership. The model set by the AAP is being followed in pieces by almost every other party. Politicos now see value in professionals entering the political space, though not all of them have ambitions of contesting for office.

One of the largest Indian political campaign machines was founded in 2013. Known at the time as the Citizens for Accountable Governance and registered as a non-profit, it was an outfit of the BJP. It was renamed after the election as the Indian Political Action Committee (IPAC), headed by Prashant Kishor. IPAC has demystified the electoral campaigning space for hundreds of young professionals who have been part of its team. For the first time on this scale, a body has given young professionals an opportunity to understand the political process from the inside through employment opportunities in a campaign machine. This knowledge will have ripple effects.

Similarly, we are seeing state governments opening up fellowship opportunities for young professionals to support bureaucrats, while parliamentarians have begun to hire 'Officers on Special Duties' to help them with research. This is not the first time that the government is opening up opportunities for young professionals to give them a close view of workings within the government. In fact, political consulting firms and opportunities to support bureaucrats and parliamentarians have existed for a while now. However, the scale at which these programmes are now opening up and the kind of talent that they are pulling in is unprecedented. The tides are shifting.

Who Is This Book For?

In a time where politics is witnessing quick shifts and there is a growing demand for professionals, it made sense to write a book that would decipher channels of entry into politics. This book has been written for two sets of audience: 1) Young, ambitious professionals who are keen on entering the political system (or are in the early stages of their political careers) and want to prepare themselves for the future, and 2) People who seek to satisfy their curiosity around politics and governance, and analyse the current political landscape better.

The book focuses on insights from my exposure to parliamentarians, especially for those aiming to be national-level leaders, as opposed to state-level legislators and regional leaders. It will be of special interest for readers running for parliamentary elections. The national focus will also interest a wider readership. You will notice that the book has stories of parliamentarians' personal experience peppered across its pages.

The book relies heavily on case-studies and narratives to ensure that there is a tangible quality to each suggestion made. I have conducted a hundred interviews or more and reviewed fifty political biographies over the course of several years to ensure my conclusions are thorough. Suitable extracts and quotes from these interviews have been presented in this book.

I also reached out to journalists, political pundits and party members (in addition to elected officials) for a comprehensive view regarding entry into the political sphere. Editors of major newspapers spoke to me about reporting and messaging during political campaigns; political advisors to chief ministers spoke about how candidates are selected; and political scientists provided insights on governance structures. Each interviewee was carefully selected keeping in mind that I wished to convey only valuable insights, and examples of regional and state leaders were included when compelling.

Finally, the writing of the book has involved a significant amount of introspection. Having spent a lifetime amidst politicians, I wanted to select experiences that were of great value. I have also brought in my opinions and experiences. For example, I have consistently seen that women have a harder time in politics and I wanted to ensure that I covered this perspective with a separate chapter. However, I have tried to stay objective and helpful for the reader. Keeping this in mind, the language and tone of the book is simple and concise.

My biggest grievance is that we have very few leaders who invest the time necessary for the study and understanding of systems of governance. We have very few leaders who are intellectually and/or professionally prepared for their roles. Several state-level surveys by media organizations show that our Members of Legislative Assembly (MLAs) do not know the difference between a parliamentarian and a legislator. Other surveys show that several parliamentarians haven't even read most legislations that they are expected to vote on. If India wants to transform as a country, we need to build on the strengths of our leadership. To support and nurture our next generation of leaders, they need to be in the know of what it takes to be a politician.

What's in This Book?

To be a successful politician, it is important that you understand political institutions, and have knowledge of how to grow in the field with adequate preparation for its ups and downs. Accordingly, this book is divided into three core sections.

The first section aims to inform the reader of the basics of political institutions. Chapters in this section throw light on the roles and responsibility of politicians and the political party systems within which a politician operates. It is critical that you understand what is expected of you as a politician, your stakeholders and what are you expected to deliver to them, and the first chapter explains the same. Responsibilities of political leaders goes beyond what we see on television and in newspapers which give us a glimpse of political leaders quibbling with one another. Most parliamentarians I have known work fourteen-hour days and divide their attention between the party, constituents and stakeholders. There is no typical day in the life of a politician, but there are some consistent expectations of them. This chapter illustrates this through examples. As you prepare yourself for your role, it is equally important that you understand the institution within which you are expected to function.

There is very little public information about the nature of political parties and how they function. Very few platforms discuss the relevance of a party to the work of a politician though it is apparent they form a key portion of the political system. The second chapter explains how political parties are relevant to a politician's career. Most politicians have to spend decades working in order to gain an in-depth view of the party system. This chapter consolidates insights and provides an overview of how political parties function. For example, recognising the party's organizational structure could be a tremendous value-addition and something each politician should be mindful of. A politician should be thoroughly aware of their party and its functioning. In addition to institutions, it is also important that one consciously builds on one's strengths. The chapter goes on to discuss how to enter politics, build a political statement and communication skills, and prepare financially for the field.

The third chapter demonstrates that most professionals bring in experiences from other fields into politics, and that each of these experiences has qualities that can add value to the political process. For example, an overwhelming number of politicians are lawyers. This is because law and politics have close ties in the framing and implementation of policy. The chapter also cites examples from other professions to illustrate skill sets that are most valued in the political field, showing professionals and students that in order to be politically relevant, it is imperative that they leverage their available skills and academic background in politics. With an understanding of how previous experience can help in entering the political arena, the following chapter focuses on communication.

Communication is pivotal to politics. The ability to speak well and communicate strong ideas will make an individual stand out in politics. The fourth chapter provides a number of examples and frameworks to aspiring politicians on how to become an effective communicator. For example, the chapter analyses Prime Minister Narendra Modi's speech in New York to point out the qualities to adopt. But communication alone is not enough.

Politics requires financial preparation. Finance is the Achilles' heel of politics. In fact, one of the biggest reasons for why people steer away from the political profession is the lack of transparency around how to make money when pursuing politics as a full-time job. Unfortunately, there has been no resolution on how to support those pursuing politics financially. If you are convinced that you want to pursue a political career, there are ways you can prepare yourself. The fifth chapter shares insights on how to manage finances when entering politics. For example, you can begin saving up and build your resume to work as a consultant. Since politics is a full-time profession, you will need to have the flexibility in your earning job. This chapter will point out ethical ways of making it in electoral politics.

It is important that as you prepare, you consider the toll that politics will take on your personal life. There are several instances of political leaders distanced from their families as they devote more and more time to their careers. However, there are enough examples to counter those experiences as well. The sixth chapter speaks about the challenges faced in balancing work with personal life. The politician's time is the public's time. But there are ways that you can manage. After all, your family and friends will be your strongest network of support as you go through the ups and downs of politics, and it is imperative that you keep them close.

The last chapter of the book is a special dedication to women. Politics is a male-dominated field. Women in politics are significantly out-numbered. Only 11 per cent of parliamentarians are women, and there are fewer women in party leadership positions. Indian society is still not progressive enough to have created an environment in which women can successfully pursue politics. Most women who try their hand in the field have their characters attacked, and others are bullied into oblivion. However, women need to stay strong and pursue politics because no society can grow without its women. And we certainly need more women in political leadership. This chapter highlights strategies on how aspiring female politicians can prepare themselves.

With the knowledge base provided in the book, you should be prepared to begin your political journey. Each chapter has been designed such that you can begin by getting a **historical perspective** of leaders who established Indian democracy (usually freedom fighters), gain an **understanding of the political landscape** on different issues, recognize a **set of characteristics** that you should aim to embody and some pointers to keep in mind as you proceed with your political career. The outline has been developed assuming that this book will serve as a reference guide to your political ambitions.

Why Should You Go into Politics?

India is at a crossroad. We have leap-frogged to a time where cell-phones and televisions have made their way to almost every household, even in the remotest regions of the country. People have access to information. They see better lives on television and on social media and aspire to those lives. With exposure, people's expectations of their political leadership have changed. This changing approach is already evident in electoral outcomes. Fortunately, we are seeing a push for the rise of a more meritocratic class of politicos.

People appreciate seeing a prime minister who hasn't inherited his post but has earned his way to the top through hard work, and a chief minister who has fought his way to the top despite being pushed around by a powerful nemesis. As the winds continue to shift, we will need not just the people's demand for a better leader, but a talented pool of people who can emerge as a promising future for the country.

For this, we need fresh blood to come into politics. Politics is a difficult career, but one of the most noble and impactful professions. If one has a desire to come in to this space, s/he should be free to do so. Knowledge of getting into politics can no longer be safeguarded by a few powerful voices in Delhi. And no longer can twelve-year-old girls be asked to come back after they have finished school and college to have their questions answered on how to enter into politics.

The winds are shifting and politics needs young and talented people like you.

SECTION I

SECTION 1

Chapter 2

What Is Politics?

A successful elected representative is a 'people's person'. From listening to constituents about their concerns; to working with party workers to ensure the presence of a strong cadre, to developing political strategies with senior leaders; an elected representative has to face varied expectations and responsibilities. Unfortunately, none of this is codified in any constitution and most political leaders have to chart their own paths. You will have to weigh out which aspect of your political responsibility you will want to prioritize. As you begin to think about a political career, it is imperative that you understand the role you are about to take on and the responsibilities attached. You must invest in studying political leadership before joining the profession. Only those who have a detailed understanding of the field are likely to succeed. You must begin by asking:

- Who is a politician?
- What does s/he do?
- What makes her/him successful?

Reading this chapter will not be enough. Your 'To do' should include:
- Reading about Indian political history and contemporary politics.

- Speaking to and learning from successful politicians
- Investing time to reflect on the kind of political leader you want to be.

Looking Back...

Bhimrao Ambedkar was born in 1891 and was the youngest of fourteen children. He was from the Mahar caste and as a Dalit, faced severe prejudice in the community. He recalled several occasions when he had to drink from a separate water fountain when travelling, being made to sit far away from his colleagues while at work, and of how he was not allowed to take money directly from the hands of the upper castes when conducting business. He spoke vividly of insults thrown at him and his family for belonging to the lower caste. However, with a father in the Indian Army, he did have one advantage: unlike other Dalits of his time, Ambedkar had access to education as part of a service rendered to all army children. He was a brilliant student.

Ambedkar completed his education with a stellar performance and eventually went on to become one of the first Dalits to attend Elphinstone College and attain higher education. He received a degree in Economics and Political Science. Eventually, he completed his doctorate on a scholarship at Columbia University in New York, one of the finest educational institutes in the world. He subsequently went on to London to get a doctorate in the Sciences. Ambedkar was nominated as a Member of the Legislative Council in 1927, where he served with tremendous success. Given how pivotal education had been to Ambedkar's career, he became a fierce advocate of access to quality education. He gained national repute during the Round Table conferences at London.

Mahatma Gandhi was to first take notice of Ambedkar, a bespectacled man fiercely advocating Dalit rights, during a Round Table conference in London. Gandhi had never met Ambedkar until then. Taken aback by his passionate speeches, Gandhi leaned over to his aide and asked, 'Who is this young man and why is he advocating Dalit rights?[1]' His aide answered, 'His name is Ambedkar and he is a Dalit himself.' Gandhi was impressed. Ambedkar eventually went on to become the father of the Constitution of India. This title was rightly earned given his detailed knowledge and academic background that gave him the skills to frame such an important document. The Indian Constitution remains the backbone of the Indian democracy.

Ambedkar's story highlights two key characteristics about the Indian political system. Firstly, the fact that people from all walks of lives have entered and thrived in Indian politics, and secondly, that Indian politics reveres those who bring with them knowledge and understanding about governance. Ambedkar's greatest weapon was his knowledge of law, politics, economics and sociology. He was a competent professional with a detailed understanding of governance. He held a degree in law, a doctorate in academics, and was a practitioner serving as a Member of the Legislative Council. This led to him being forever embedded in Indian history as the father of the Indian Constitution.

Throughout Indian political history, men and women with a deep understanding of governance systems have stood out. The individual might understand governance through an engaged study of communities while travelling across the country, or be able to astutely analyse Indian history and

[1] Carnegie Endowment, *A New Normal in Indian Politics*, a podcast, 12 March 2016.

politics being a historian or political scientist with an in-depth knowledge of the past.

While you don't have to walk the path that Ambedkar did in dedicating your life to understanding governance, it is important that you have an understanding of the political system. This chapter is devoted to explaining what it means to be a politician and should serve as a basis for you to begin engaging with, learning about and probing the Indian governance space.

Learn the Basics

Like any other profession, the first step of becoming a politician requires an understanding of the job and its demands.

Who is a politician?

In western democracies, a nationally elected political leader is responsible for representing the people on policy matters in parliament. However, parliamentarians in Indian democracy juggle multiple fronts that range between grieving constituents, disgruntled party workers, angry media outlets, vested interest groups and demanding senior party leaders. Even though each politician maintains a different lifestyle to balance all these priorities, they recognize that interacting with people from different walks of life, including the party, are a core aspect of their work. Ultimately, a politician is somebody who **understands**, **connects and resolves** the issues of her/his constituents, party members and external stakeholders.

A few years ago, I had the opportunity to shadow a senior minister and party spokesperson to understand how he spent his day. I was amazed with his schedule which was as follows:

WHAT IS POLITICS?

7:00 a.m. – 9:00 a.m.: Review cabinet notes and ensure important papers are signed
Purpose: Be an efficient minister

9:00 a.m. – 11:30 a.m.: Meeting with party worker to understand condition in constituency. Main questions to ask:
- How are party workers doing on the ground?
- Are there any issues with the opposition leader?
- Is there any disgruntlement in the local party cadre?
- Are party membership levels stable?

Purpose: Maintain a connection with party members on the ground

11: 30 a.m. – 1:30 p.m.: Meet with constituents (who have prior appointments). Most requests will revolve around:
- Admission to government hospitals
- Entrance to government schools/colleges
- Request for financial support for family members (for marriage, hospital admission, etc.)
- Confirming rail tickets
- Government job requests for children or family members (in overwhelming numbers)
- Private job requests (a few)

Purpose: Maintain a strong reputation with constituents

1:30 p.m. – 2:30 p.m.: Lunch meeting with a business leader or prominent person.
Purpose: Stay connected with prospective 'influencers'

3:00 p.m. – 6:30 p.m.: Meeting with senior bureaucrats to understand:
- Major policy issues communicated by stakeholders
- Bottlenecks in the ministry
- Pending work on the minister's end

- Presentation on upcoming programmes

Purpose: Be an efficient minister

7:00 p.m. – 9:00 p.m.: Meeting with party leader at his residence to discuss:
- Upcoming state elections (and roles and responsibilities)
- Party strategy and messaging
- Possible candidates and leaders for respective select states
- Updates on any state issues (as deemed appropriate)

Purpose: Ensure a strong standing within the party and continue to maintain strong relationships with leaders.

9:00 p.m. – 10:30 p.m.: Appearing on various news channels to speak about the party's stance.

Purpose: Ensure that there remains visibility about work.

After completing his last commitment, the minister would either return to his residence in Central Delhi around 11:00 p.m. or head over to the party leader's house. Discussions on party strategy would continue till around 1:00 a.m. The politician had maintained this lifestyle for close to four years by that time. At the end his term, he took a month long vacation to meditate.

Successful politicians often spend entire days listening to people and their problems, trying to help them when they can. Whether it is dealing with a constituent looking for railway tickets or senior party members proposing a membership drive, the most successful politicians need to be good listeners and efficient problem solvers.

What makes a good listener?

Most of us struggle with the ability to sit quietly and listen to people. We are tempted to interrupt others while listening and are likely to compete to put in our two bits. Most often these interruptions are fuelled either by the desire to finish the conversation and come to a quick resolution, or to express an opinion that has been on our mind passionately. A good listener, however, doesn't cut people off. S/he allows the person speaking to pour out their emotions and thoughts in their entirety and provides input, if any, only at the end. You must have noticed that a number of politicians nod their heads in agreement quietly, with the occasional facial expression: this is evidence of their practice in listening. Here are some of the traits that would make you a good listener:

- Make sure the other person has finished what they are saying (you can do so by counting to five to yourself once the person pauses)
- Ensure they are not pausing, but are finished.
- Do NOT interrupt
- When they are done talking, briefly summarize their concerns and THEN propose solutions
- Do not commit to a solution unless you are certain that you can fulfil it.

Being a good listener is an art and requires significant practice. Practice this skill at every opportunity you get.

What does a politician do?

It is hard to pin down the responsibility of a politician. The Indian Constitution does not codify a politician's responsibilities and neither do political parties. In fact, most of us piece together the role of a parliamentarian through what we read in newspapers or hear in discussions. Several random question-and-answer sessions with elected officials have proven that even they have a limited understanding of the role.

Interestingly, our education system is not combatting these situations either. While our civics books teach us what the Lok Sabha and Rajya Sabha are supposed to do, there is no mention of the role of the parliamentarian who are running these houses. The lack of a defined responsibility for a parliamentarian often means that they try to work on everything under the sun. While each defines their own scope of work, most parliamentarians maintain a common set of stakeholders. They are as follows:

Constituents: In the Indian democratic context, parliamentarians rely on voters to bring them back into office. Therefore, they spend significant amounts of time with the constituent, i.e., voters who have the power to re-elect them. Members of Parliament (MPs) listen to their problems and help when possible. With public service systems broken in most parts of the country, constituents turn to their elected representatives to avail basic facilities like law and order, and sanitation. This is unlike several western democracies where parliamentarians focus on policy making. In fact, the introduction of the Local Area Development Fund for MPs has institutionalized the expectation that parliamentarians will provide developmental support to the community. The Local Area Development Fund was initiated at the request of parliamentarians where an allocation of five crores is provided to each MP by the Ministry of Programme Implementation that s/he can then spend on initiatives that are found to be of importance. Parliamentarians often go beyond these five crores and mobilize resources through Corporate Social Responsibility (CSR) to implement development projects in their communities.

'A politician has many avatars,' explains Dinesh Trivedi, a Lok Sabha Member from Barrackpore, West Bengal, and ex-Railway Minister. 'One night around 2 a.m., I heard my phone ring. I looked at the caller ID and couldn't recognize the number. I wondered who could call me so late but being an MP felt, that I should answer the call in case it were urgent. I picked up the phone. "Hello," a shrill voice answered from the other side. "Dinesh Babu," he continued, raising his voice. "Yes," I answered, trying to wash away the sleepiness from my voice.'

'"Dineshji, my wife has run away! She left me a note saying so," the man continued. I didn't understand why he was calling me. I wanted to tell him "Well, she hasn't run away with me," but I maintained my decorum and said "How can I be of any help?" The man answered, "I need you to call the police now and lodge a complaint for me."'

Trivedi continued narrating the story as he sank in a chair, as though the cardinal truth of being a politician had finally dawned on him. 'When you are elected to office, the constituent knows full well that his vote has gotten you there and that you are at their service. If you are thinking about politics, be prepared to serve the people because they will call upon you and you must help them in any way. Your accessibility and support to your constituents defines your leadership capacity,' he finished. Most elected officials prioritize the constituent, the primary stakeholder.

Constituents are even more important when you are vying for a ticket to contest for office. Political parties like the Congress and the Bharatiya Janta Party (BJP) require a grassroots presence before giving a politician a ticket. While there is no concrete indicator for measuring what is considered a community connect, one thing is evident: most political leaders would expect you to have some name recognition within community members and evidence that people believe you enough to work on your campaign and vote for you.

Kamal Nath, a senior Congress leader and ex-cabinet minister explains this further to me. 'A party like Congress would ask itself,"if person X has to go door to door for voters, will they be received well enough?"' A prospective voter or constituent is very important in the career of an elected representative and thus s/he spends significant time in wooing them.

Party: The party is the backbone for most politicians. As you will read in later chapters, the party provides each candidate with the basic infrastructure in the form of people, a captured voter base and ideology. Party tickets can often decide the fate of a politician and therefore, in addition to the constituent, politicians are also accountable to the party itself.

P.D. Rai, the Lok Sabha Member from Sikkim, joined the Sikkim Democratic Front (SDF) when he heard Pawan Chamling talk for the first time. He was tired of the corrupt ways of previous leaders and was excited about a new man with a vision. Given his IIT-IIM background, Rai joined the party's communication team. He wrote countless white papers, policy documents, journals and briefs. Rai was made responsible for interfacing with the media, developing the core message for the party, and ensuring that party members were communicated a consistent message. The leadership saw the value he was bringing and proposed him as the candidate for the Lok Sabha election. In 2009, with the support of a party that had a strong worker base in the grassroots, Rai came into the Lok Sabha.

Even though Rai's responsibilities have increased since then, he continues to lead the SDF's communications work, in addition to being the face of the party in Delhi. In 2014, for example, Rai had organized a major event in partnership with the UN in Sikkim to launch the Human Development Report that got him significant accolades within the party.

The political party plays a monumental role in a politician's career. Giving a political aspirant a ticket to securing election funding, a party can be a game changer for politicians. This is not just the case for Lok Sabha politicians but also for those in the Rajya Sabha.

In 2016, Maharashtra held municipal elections in several major cities. The Modi wave seemed to be crushing regional parties during this time. A leader from one of the regional parties approached the senior leadership and promised them a majority victory. In return, he asked to be 'rewarded appropriately.' The local leader worked tirelessly against the Modi wave to win the support of the public, eventually bringing back a majority of the seats. He was rewarded with a Rajya Sabha seat. The party leadership decides the fate of leaders and often watches the activities of their members. Therefore, it is important to maintain close connection with the party.

Parliament: Unfortunately, the Indian Constitution doesn't have the teeth to ensure that parliamentarians are conducting their policy responsibilities efficiently. There are no repercussions that parliamentarians face for failing to attend sessions, or refusing to partake in discussion or refusing to attend standing committee meetings (which are policy drafting bodies consisting of MPs). When parliament fails to function, headlines in newspapers talk about the inefficiency of national leaders, and when parliamentarians create a ruckus, newspapers name and shame individuals.

During elections, an MP's role becomes even more prominent. Take, for example, the general elections of 2014 when major news channels like NDTV and Times Now had developed report cards to rank politicians by their attendance in the parliament and the questions they asked, and about MP Local Area Development Funds allocated. News channels repeatedly showcased these report cards and discussed the performance of MPs.

The media attention around the parliament has required MPs to be more conscious of their performance. Some MPs like Vijay Darda have gone so far as to publish all of the questions that he has asked in parliament in a book. It is now more important for MPs to be effective policy makers.

Other Stakeholders: Astute politicians often make a conscious decision to build and maintain connections beyond their party and constituency. They recognize that they may face situations where they will have to call in favours. They develop friendships with lawyers, doctors, journalists and business people. The most efficient politicians are great networkers who have in their Rolodex people from all walks of life.

Basics of networking

Networking is critical for the survival of any politician. Simply put, it is an individual's ability to meet with people from all walks of life and be able to cultivate a relationship of trust and confidence. Indians don't look at networking favourably since it is often related to nepotism. However, as a politician,

WHAT IS POLITICS?

you will have to have the capacity to call in favours and help people out.

The rules of networking are seemingly simple, but difficult to execute because they require patience and follow-ups. The way to begin the networking process is by:

- Going to public events like dinners, conferences and speaking engagements.
- Reaching out to new people at public events in an effort to learn from them and/or share your own experiences that might be of value to them.
- Exchange contact information and follow-up with them after the initial connect.
- Make sure to meet with them and continue to stay in touch.
- Do not disregard anyone because you don't share their background or area of interest.

Networking allows for you to build a cohort of trusted friendships and relationships that you can call upon later. Established politicians, like MPs, who already have several deep networks, are masters at networking. They ensure that they are in touch with the right people by doing small things like throwing a party in Delhi during the parliament sessions.

In these parties, one notices that the MP has invited not just other political colleagues but also journalists, doctors, lawyers, police officers, scientists, business leaders and people from almost every imaginable profession. These MPs recognize that it is important that they remain connected to a diverse set of individuals so that they can learn from them and call on them in case they need any support.

One case I saw was of an astute politician and a three-time MP who had fallen out of favour with the party leader after he had made some unexpected comments against the party leadership. Soon enough, he was not invited to attend leadership meetings, the communications team stopped sending him to news channel interviews, and party loyalists had stopped calling him. He needed to create value for himself but was unsure how that might be possible.

The AAP was quickly rising to its peak at this point. He rode on their backs. The MP called up a few of his friends in the media and informed them that the AAP had called and asked him to join the leadership, but that he was contemplating whether or not to leave his party given his loyalties to them. There was not much substance to what he was saying. Over the new few days, he cultivated this rumour, until it came out in the public as a story.

He pushed for the news to be picked up by other television channels. Though they were hesitant at first, they honoured their relationship with him and ran a show on it. The article reached the ears of his party members. The party felt insecure about losing a senior leader and suddenly, the politician was back in the party's 'good books.'

In the case discussed above, the politician had strong ties to the media and used them to bring himself back to good faith with the party. In other situations, like elections, a politician might need to draw upon close friends to get donations to fund their campaign.

As you can see, a public leader is answerable to several stakeholders and her/his daily life involves constant juggling between them. One of the key takeaways for aspiring politicians from this is to work on tackling multiple actors in your life. While most of us think our colleagues, friends and family are a full palette, an aspiring politician has to be prepared to work with many more actors than just this much.

A politician is a people's person.

What makes a politician successful?

As you consider entering politics, you might be keen to adopt personality traits that will make you amenable to success. Fortunately, India has all kinds of public leaders. It has those who are ambitious and outgoing, those who are tactful and reserved, and those in between. Despite diversity in leadership styles and approaches, some elements remain consistent in what successful politicians maintain. Having met and worked with politicians, I would strongly recommend the following top five characteristics.

1. Dedication to public service: Whether it is pursuing a Public Interest Litigation (PIL), helping poor people find the right medical help, or campaigning for student's rights, successful political leaders view their work as a way to help the poorest of the poor and those in need. They are dedicated to public service. 'Constituents recognize the dedication to service and often reward us during elections,' shares Rajeev Satav, Lok Sabha MP from Hingoli, who rose to politics through student activism.

   Successful politicians often take varied ways to make an impact on their constituents. Take, for example, Rabindra Kumar Jena, a successful businessperson who transitioned to politics in 2014. As the director of Balasore Mining and Alloys, Jena was swamped by people in his community for jobs and health support. He did not shy away from these demands and helped hundreds of people, forming a wing within his office to tend to the needs of those who came in to meet him. In 2016, he won the Lok Sabha seat from his constituency of Balasore, Odisha, having made a name as a people's person. Since coming in to office, he increased his commitment to working for the people significantly.

While the party and external stakeholders remain a priority for politicians, this does not deter them from wanting to benefit the poor. It is important for aspiring politicians to see their primary and core purpose as being public service. This focus has not just brought success to the individual but also strengthened our governance systems.

2. Acumen for emotional intelligence: A successful politician is not just intelligent but emotionally aware of the sentiments and responses of the individuals s/he meets. 'There was a charm in Indira Gandhi. If you watched her during the elections carefully, as I did, you would notice that she made it a point to go shake people's hands and walk through crowds. She did that intentionally to make people feel that she was not above them but with them. And consciously built the brand that even in her perfectly worn saree, she was, in fact, one of the poor and could feel their pains and joys,' a senior journalist who had travelled extensively with Indira Gandhi shared with me. 'She knew, for example, that it is more important to listen to people and make them feel that their voices matter, than anything else… in the case of Indira Gandhi, she valued it more than even doing something for the people,' he continued.

The journalists' stories highlighted the importance of maintaining a high level of emotional intelligence. Emotional intelligence involves sentiments and thoughts that often overpower our logic and drive decision making. Given how much our politics is run on emotion, successful political leaders need to be able to gauge emotions and respond appropriately. It helps to be a keen observer of human emotions and studying the responses of people around to gain an understanding of the prospective drivers for decision making. These will help you hone your emotional intelligence.

3. Perseverance and Resilience: When you meet any MP and convey to them your desire to enter politics, they will at first express disapproval. Most will say that failure is synonymous with politics. Don't be discouraged, because all politicians who tell you it is difficult have probably reached some level of success. Nonetheless, prepare to have your patience tested.

'I had been working in the Congress party back-office for seven years before I got a chance to work in mainstream politics,' Jairam Ramesh explained. 'I was managing policy work and had a small team who supported me with research. You have to be patient and support your party through any needs,' he extrapolated. Most political stories begin in party offices, or with work as party workers. Those who are determined, stay within their role and ensure that they are able to demonstrate a distinct value addition. It often takes politicians several years to be able to successfully establish their credibility in the space and contest for office.

Remember that doggedness is the name of the game.

4. Each step of the process requires some level of risk – joining politics, choosing a party, backing the right party leader and contesting for election. You never know if the party you have joined might disown you because of a statement you made, or if the party leader you have been backing is expelled, or if your election

funders back out because of financial concerns. Politics seeks only those who have a risk-taking appetite.

Consider, for example, Mamata Banerjee's career when she decided to back the Congress party and a violent CPI(M) party member was keen on eliminating her. She had her skull fractured, body brutally bruised, and was dragged out of the chief minister's office by her hair and attacked with machetes. She continued to battle the ruling party for over a decade before she finally came in to power. Banerjee and her followers have cited more than one example of when she was close to being killed. Though Banerjee's case might be extreme, it is telling that politics is about taking risks. If you are considering a career in politics, recognize that time and again you will be taking risks and that you have to have the temperament to do so.

5. Intellectual adventurers: The general impression that people maintain about elected officials is that they are ignorant leaders who have little idea about the world and its functioning. Take, for example, how Smriti Irani was mocked when she had said that she had a degree from Yale, or how shocked people were when Lalu Yadav was invited to the Harvard India Conference as one of the lead speakers. This idea that leaders are ignorant is completely incorrect.

Successful politicians are those who have thought about, learned about and reflected on various issues. In fact, most prominent leaders from Jairam Ramesh to P. Chidamabaran are prolific writers (in later chapters you will notice that writing is a source of income for most politicians in the making). Atal Bihari Vajpayee has several writings to his credit, including poetry. There is no dearth of writers among political leaders.

Given the recent requirement to be well-versed in international events and culture, it is important to gain worldly experience. Consider how Narendra Modi during his tenure with the RSS took up the opportunity to travel across India, and later internationally as prime minister. Being able to meet with various people gives you the cutting edge to be able to understand various cultures and take an inward look at various issues.

Successful politicians are constantly seeking to learn new things and traveling, reading and writing are a key part of that. Whether they appear to be so or not, successful politicians are intellectual adventurers and you too must seek to embrace this characteristic.

While there might be other characteristics that might exist amongst successful politicians, these are few that are woven across almost all of them. As an aspiring politician you must be open to constantly seeking the strong qualities of politicians and trying to imbibe them.

Food for Thought: India's Political Narrative

When you think about politics, what are the first images that you conjure in your mind? It is likely that you either think about the greedy, corrupt and uneducated leader, or the selfless, committed and grounded leader. Unfortunately, very few of us immediately conjure up a middle class, well-educated person who has worked in the professional world who could lead with confidence. The issue with our images is that both of these perspectives represent people from extremes.

Our current political narrative places a strong preference on the Gandhian lifestyle and puts a taboo on any financial income from politics. 'When I was young, a politician was a farmer or businessman who took a few years off to serve in public office. And after his term, went back to his regular job,' explained a senior businessman who is a civil society leader. However, focusing only on a Gandhian leader leaves out several talented professionals who could be phenomenal as leaders. Countries that do not maintain such a narrative often do better in governance.

For example, the prime minister in Singapore has a salary of over thirty lakh dollars, much of it dependent on her/his performance in office. In the years that the country does not fare as well, their salary is cut. Similarly, the president of the United States (US) has a salary of four lakh dollars. With such a salary, the president can lead a comfortable life and not feel vulnerable about what the future holds for them. In India, however, the basic salary of a politician is fairly low, especially in comparison to their counterparts in other countries. Expectations that anyone would work a sixteen-hour day on a low salary is unrealistic. However, we continue to maintain the expectation of a selfless political leader.

If as citizens we expect to have more educated professionals come in to the political sphere, we have to be more realistic about the narrative we weave. As future politicians, it is important that you engage in discourse on the need to have proper compensation and qualities attached to political leaders. For example, it is alright if a political leader has a family, and it is also alright if s/he thinks about where to garner financial resources from. Unless we put in place a realistic image of who a future politician can be, it will be hard to bring in talented and educated professionals to the political space.

Interestingly, some amends are now being made and we are starting to realize that we need to move away from common historical narratives of who can be a public leader and look towards who we need to as public leaders in this hour. The likes of Arvind Kejriwal and Devendra Fadnavis are emerging as young, dynamic and educated people who demonstrate a strong interest in serving the public. These chapters hope to involve even more people as part of this changing narrative and usher in a generation of talented and passionate public leaders.

Books to read:
I highly recommend you read the following books to get a better understanding about Indian politics:
1. *Indian Constitution* published by Oxford University Press
2. NCERT Class VIII Civics textbook
3. NCERT Class IX Civics textbook
4. *India After Gandhi: The History of the World's Largest Democracy* by Ramchandra Guha
5. *Cut-Outs, Caste and Cine Stars: The World of Tamil Politics* by Vaasanthi
6. *Oxford Companion to Indian Politics*
7. *India: A Portrait* by Patrick French
8. *Half-Lion: How P.V Narasimha Rao Transformed India* by Vinay Sitapati

Chapter 3

What Is a Political Party?

Political parties are institutions within which politicians function. Established political parties offer candidates a well-defined ideology that resonates with the masses, a team of grassroot-level workers to help with campaigns, and limited financial resources to spend during election. A party hopes to have enough candidates win elections so that they can form a government. The strength of a political party lies in how many of their candidates win. Despite the seemingly straightforward nature of this work, the functioning of political parties remains nebulous.

There are hardly any details about what happens within a party, including information on internal hierarchies and decision-making processes. Interestingly though, most political parties have common structures and operations that are implicit for all party members to follow. Politicians who have been a member of political parties for a while can identify these characteristics. Successful politicians work within these structures and rise up. They recognize skilsets that are valued within the party and tap in to them. As you begin planning your political journey, it is important that you learn the following:

- What is a political party? How does a party fit in to a politician's career?

- How is a political party structured? Who are its various stakeholders?
- What kind of skill-sets do a political party value? How do you get noticed by senior party leaders?
- How does a party decide on electoral candidates?

Reading this chapter will not be enough. Your 'To do' should include reaching out to politicians and
- Understanding their experiences with various political parties
- Reading up on party history and ideology
- Reflecting on what your value addition to any political party will be

Evaluate which political party you will fit into best and begin networking within those parties.

Looking Back...

Ashutosh was a talented lawyer. He was a fierce believer in equal treatment. On one occasion, when a British soldier threw out Ashutosh's shoes for no good reason, he retaliated by throwing out the British soldier's coat. Ashutosh raised his son, Syama Prasad, to follow these principles. Syama Prasad was born on 6 July 1901, and followed his father's footsteps.[2]

Syama Prasad Mookherjee was an exceptional academic, one of the youngest vice-chancellor's of Calcutta University. He went on to become a successful politician. He was a Member of the Legislative Council and Legislative Assembly (MLA). Throughout his career, he believed in equal opportunity for all. However, in 1939, Syama saw injustice: A Muslim cluster

[2] Das, S.C., *The Biography of Bharat Kesri Dr. Syama Prasad Mookerjee with Modern Implications*, New Delhi: Abhinav Publications, 2003.

had openly pillaged, raped and killed Bengali Hindus. The British and the Congress watched in silence. As a people's representative, he saw how the government was failing its Hindu population. He joined the Hindu Mahasabha that year.

Over the next several years, Syama Prasad Mookherjee travelled across the country as a member of the Hindu Mahasabha. He planned festivals and organized functions and grew closer to his fellow members, establishing his identity as a hard-working and committed individual. In 1944, his credibility within the Mahasabha led him to be elected its president. As a leader, his leaning towards building a Hindu nation became stronger. His experiences helped him define his own political ideology.

In 1946, the Noakhali riots left over 6,000 dead and this altered Syama Prasad Mookherjee's views forever. He read the riots as being a result of the Muslim minority oppressing the Hindu majority. As president of the Hindu Mahasabha, he travelled across Bengal and listened to thousands of stories of the suffering Hindu majority. He saw the need for India to treat its citizens equally. As time passed, his religious affiliations grew and so did his political influence.

In independent India, Nehru offered Syama Prasad Mookherjee the position of Minister for Industry and Supply. He served a short term since disagreements between him and Nehru arose on issues of how to work with Pakistan. He resigned in 1950. He quit his ministerial position but was keen on continuing his political journey.

Mookherjee had gained extensive experience of how to run large volunteer-based organizations with a strong ideology because of his work with the Hindu Mahasabha. However, forming a political party needed a national presence. He recognized that his presence was limited to West Bengal.

He turned to Guru Golwalkar, the head of Rashtriya Swayamsewak Sangh (RSS), for counsel. He shared his vision for an India that treated Hindus and Muslims equally. L.K. Advani cited this as being one of the most important meetings in India's political history.

Golwalkar offered Syama Prasad Mookherjee support in the form of human capital. He told him that in order to start a political party, he would need workers willing to campaign for the cause of a Hindu nation across India. He offered the support of RSS workers who could help build the party. RSS bases were present across the country and were the perfect entity to initiate the party. With the support of Guru Golwalkar, Syama Prasad Mookherjee founded the Bharatiya Jan Sangh, the predecessor of the Bharatiya Janata Party (BJP).

The tie-ups with RSS coupled with the current socio-political context of Partition had given the Bharatiya Jan Sangh a significant push. Syama Prasad Mookherjee had identified an ideology that resonated with the masses, access to a worker base willing to campaign door-to-door and the brand affiliation of the RSS. The deep-rooted practice of RSS workers campaigning for BJP continues even today because at the core, a Hindu nation has remained a consistent vision through the party's evolution.

The story of Syama Prasad Mookherjee and the founding of Bharatiya Jan Sangh highlight the historical role of identity politics in India. Every successful Indian political party in India has been born out of the mobilization of a marginalized or angered population who feels they face discrimination. For Syama Prasad Mookherjee, this group were Hindus who felt neglected during Partition. Other parties have tapped into ethnic or regional sentiments, as you will see later in the chapter. As our democracy has matured, parties have systematically perfected this art of reaching out and seeking the vote of a religious or ethnic group and created a strong culture of *identity politics*.

Explanation: What is a political party?

Every morning, newspapers remind us of the gamut of activities that political parties engage in. From protesting outside the houses of chief ministers to walking out in parliament to campus vigils, a political parties' breadth of work has only grown with time. But what is a political party responsible for? How does making noise and disrupting governance really help any political party? The simplest way for thinking of a political party is to compare it to a company that sells a specific product. A political party is an entity that **sells** ideas about the best way to be governed in exchange for votes. The more noise they make about their own idea and thinking, putting down the failure of other ideas and thought, the more likely they feel they will grab citizens' attention, and eventually their votes. If you think about it critically, you will see that a political party offers:

A Product: The ideology about the best way that people can be governed. For the AAP, the product is a corruption-free India, for the Communist party of India (Marxist) (CPI(M) it is an equitable society for the most vulnerable, and for the Bahujan Samajwadi Party (BSP) it is about protecting Dalits and vulnerable communities. Each political party has defined a path for governance in order to build the strongest country. In their party constitution, manifesto and literature, they identify their ideology in more detail. Almost every party promises that if the country were to follow their ideology, we will grow and prosper as a nation. Interestingly though, ideology has lost its charm over time, and parties have shifted their focus to promising tangible development promises, like houses and jobs. Political parties are convinced that voters are pulled in more by these promises than an ideology.

Employees: The people who work to produce and sell the political ideology. A district-level worker goes door-to-door to advertise political ideology to potential customers, i.e., voters; a party's senior leadership develops and hones the political message by gauging the pulse of the people framing the right message; and the political candidate is the salesperson of the party who aims to assemble large crowds and make a pitch to them about the plan to roll out the ideology. The employees are key to the success of any political party. The party members decide the fate of the political party. So even though all political parties are volunteer-based, it is imperative that the leadership thinks more carefully about the kind of talent that they are recruiting.

Customer: The voter 'buys' the product with their votes. The vote is currency in politics and elections are like a market assembled for the sale of ideology in exchange for votes. Political parties are responsible for developing a sound product that is well-advertised through party workers and candidates. Those who are able to develop and launch a sound product that resonates with the masses, end up getting a vote. However, those who fail to do so end up losing elections.

Much like companies, political parties also need to be mindful about the product that they are selling and the human capital that they are employing to market these products. For example, if each party had consciously mapped out specific community leaders to organize road shows and women leaders to bring together women's groups and young leaders to put together rallies in a structured and strategic way, then there would be a lot more traction. Unfortunately, even national elections go into full swing only a month in advance of elections. Most processes are haphazard. With over forty and fifty registered parties contesting national elections, there is stiff competition and parties need to be better prepared. Unfortunately, political parties don't share the professionalism and structured thought of private sector firms!

Another prominent example of identity politics is the creation of the Bahujan Samajwadi Party (BSP) by Kanshi Ram. Kanshi Ram faced discrimination when he was a student in Pune. He noticed that upper castes dominated Indian politics and that there was no space for vulnerable castes and communities within it. He identified the need for a Dalit voice that would champion the Dalit cause. He left his job to start a campaign against Dalit discrimination. Over the course of two decades, he eagerly sought out the Dalit voter base and built an ideology around the need to have Dalit representation.

He went door-to-door signing people up for party membership, holding road shows and rallies and speaking to Dalits who felt discriminated. He built his ideology around a voter group that he recognized could be mobilized. He gained his reputation within the Dalit community. As he cultivated this movement, he heard that a young Dalit woman named Mayawati had spoken passionately about Dalit rights. He needed a face beyond his own. He recruited her to further the goal of the party. Mayawati and Kanshi Ram became the public face of the Dalit movement in the political sphere.

Kanshi Ram had brilliantly identified the untapped demographic of Dalits who could become a voter group. He saw that no one was exclusively catering to the Dalit population and that formed a major chunk of the population, enough to form its own party. He perfected his messaging and built trust and unity in the community over twenty years, meeting with people across India and listening to their concerns.

Eventually the message resonated and the BSP came in to power in Uttar Pradesh. The BSP today is one of the leading national parties in the country, reaching out to all vulnerable castes and groups, promising to be their voice. What Kanshi Ram did with Dalits, other leaders have done with different communities, i.e., mobilized them on the basis of identity.

From Jats in Haryana to Kurmis in Bihar, each major caste, religious or ethnic group has been mobilized by a regional or national political party. In each instance, a party has promised that those who have felt marginalized will have their voices heard. As an election promise, such sentiments have cropped up time and again. In fact, Indian political parties during election rallies often explicitly state the demographic whose vote they hope to get, and tailor message to appeal to them.

This is very unlike the nature of western democracies. In the US, for example, ideological stances define political parties. For example, the Democratic Party has a left-of-centre stance, are socially progressive and believe that big government must support the socially vulnerable. The Republic Party is right-of-centre, believes in open markets and a small government. In the US, the voter groups the party appeals to does not define the party.

Political parties in India base themselves on identity groups. Listed below is a breakdown of some political parties and the voter groups that they have explicitly appealed to:

TABLE 1: Major Indian parties and their target demography

Name of Party	Target Demography
Bharatiya Janta Party	Hindus and the middle class
Bahujan Samaj Party	Dalits
Trinamool Congress	Anti-CPI(M) citizens
Aam Aadmi Party	'Anti-corruption' and the middle class
Shiromani Akali Dal	Powerful Sikhs bodies and those supported by SGPC and DSGMC
AIADMK	The rural poor and unorganized workers (originally aimed at non-Brahmin voters)
DMK	Urban and organized workers and the middle-class
CPI (M)	Workers' Unions (urban), SC/ST, the poor (any marginalized community)
Samajwadi Party	Muslims in UP, the Yadavs (and other upper caste Hindus)
Telegu Desam Party	Kamma caste and the Andhra regional identity
Telangana Rashtra Samiti	Those wanting a separate state from Andhra Pradesh
Shiv Sena	Marathi speakers
Naga People's Front	Indigenous Naga communities

As you can see from the sample of political parties above, each has a core voter group that they appeal to. The notable exception within the group is the Indian National Congress (INC), the oldest political party that has an evolving nature. Depending on the time frame, the INC, also known as Congress, has appealed to varying voter groups. For example, under Indira Gandhi, the Congress appealed to the poor, whereas under Sonia Gandhi, the party appealed to backward castes and minority groups. The Congress is an anomaly in that it does not have a fixed voter group.

As you think about which political party appeals to you, it is important that you consider the voter base they are targeting and if you are comfortable with working in that context. Identity and voter base are key to a party's functioning and therefore it must be a significant component of your decision-making as well. Do you feel that you have a strong Hindu identity? Do you feel close to your caste and community? Are you more secular in your perspective? Party workers who you will surround yourself with will embody those sentiments and it is important that you ask yourself these questions.

Even though there is much discourse and documentation about political parties as larger entities, there is very little discussion about what happens to the individual politician when s/he joins a political party. Having interviewed over a hundred politicians (and met many others), I have found that very few politicians discuss how they climbed up the ranks within parties and came to the notice of senior leadership. In fact, most politicians tend to skip over details of their activities within the party and focus on the narrative after they joined parliament. Nonetheless, it is very important for aspiring politicians to understand *how an individual rises within the party structure to gain prominence.* The upcoming section of the book aims to decipher the internal functioning of political parties.

How Does a Political Party Work?

If I am an aspiring consultant and I go to a partner at one of the top-consulting firms, s/he would be able to spell out the path to becoming a partner at the firm. 'Go to business school, solve consulting case-studies for interviews, join as an analyst or associate, commit yourself to your work and follow your manager,' would be few of the steps that s/he might highlight. If I go to a political leader and ask her/him how I could eventually rise up within the political party rank, I am unlikely to get any such detail. In fact, most political leaders would just say, 'Join the party,' and then it would be a dead end. One of the reasons that such a nebulous state exists is because, arguably, political leaders want to hoard power. However, that should not concern you. You should focus on understanding the party and how you can rise within it.

Through conversations with members from several political parties, I have been able to draw up the following 'organizational chart' that most political parties maintain. This chart will give you an idea about how parties function and what the different wings within them are and within which of

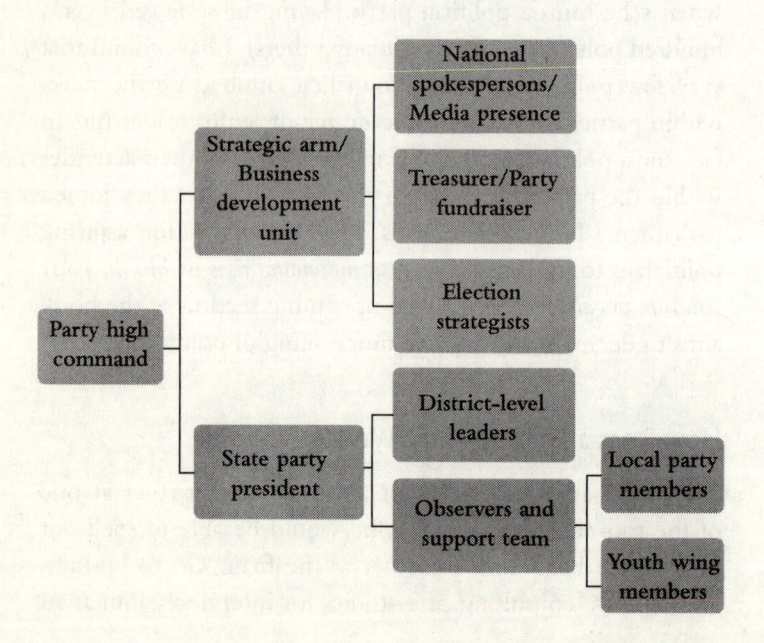

```
Party high command
├── Strategic arm/Business development unit
│   ├── National spokespersons/Media presence
│   ├── Treasurer/Party fundraiser
│   └── Election strategists
└── State party president
    ├── District-level leaders
    └── Observers and support team
        ├── Local party members
        └── Youth wing members
```

WHAT IS A POLITICAL PARTY?

these you can see yourself. The political party you join might not have these specific structures, but they will certainly have similar stakeholders.

Most political aspirants begin with the party base (that consists of members of the youth wing and local party members). The party base is made up of **grassroots party workers**, i.e., the foot soldiers who are responsible for executing party programmes in specific geographies. A grassroots worker is often embedded in a district so that s/he can spread the word about the party and its goals. S/he is responsible for organizing events, like rallies and protests. A base worker is likely to leverage her/his social standing in the community to get traction for a political party. S/he tends to be either a community member or a youth wing member, though anybody can become a grassroots member. Grassroots workers begin to get noticed when they visibly bring on new board members or voter bases for the party (details are listed in the next section).

Rabia Kidwai is an example of a local party worker in Delhi. Kidwai recognized her ambition to run for political office during her teens. Subsequently, she deferred her college admissions to join the Congress as a party worker. Kidwai says that there is no 'typical' day as a full-time party worker. However, she does spend considerable amount of time on any given day interacting with party colleagues and planning programmes and events to increase the party's visibility. On the day I spoke to her, she was working on executing a Congress rally. She was responsible for logistics and ensured that there was sufficient transportation to bus the audience to the rally.

Kidwai explained that it was important for her to show unquestioned commitment to furthering the party's cause. Only then, she believed, would the party consider promoting her within the ranks. If Kidwai were to be promoted, she would become a district leader. Since Kidwai is working in Delhi, she might be given the position of party leader of the South Delhi region.

The second rung of leadership in a party consists of **district-level leaders**. District leaders are responsible for planning, executing and monitoring a party's activities within a district. They are the eyes and ears for the senior party leadership on the ground. Party leaders often make an effort to travel across the state to identify promising young men and women who can pull in mass support, and promote them to district leadership. Most party workers plan on dedicating a few years to ground work and then rising up to a district leadership position.

A district leader becomes particularly important during an election. Most district leaders are given the task of running a successful campaign for the candidate and work closely with the candidate to ensure victory. A district leader might have the title of a District President, Observer or District Spokesperson, depending on the political party.

During the West Bengal elections of 2016, Mamata Banerjee made it a point to reach out to every district president across the state. 'I want you to win me the election. Work closely with your candidate and understand what your workers and your constituents want. Plan rallies and events accordingly. Get me the election,' she urged each one of them. She valued the role of district leadership so much so that she handpicked district leaders, placing them in positions that would bring in the strongest value.

In some states, party leaders are turning to young people for district leadership roles. Twenty-six-year-old Manali from the Nationalist Congress Party (NCP) was given the responsibility of bringing in young women's votes in the Pune Municipal Election of 2017. 'I was a member of the Yuvati (young women's organization) for the NCP. I would travel across the state and connect with young women to understand their problems. I organized counselling melas, professional coaching sessions and other events to provide opportunities for young women. The party leadership noticed my work and felt that I was adding value. Supriya Sule and Ajit Pawar soon gave me the responsibility of managing the women's vote in the Municipal elections,' she said to me with pride. Manali is seen as an upcoming leader within the NCP. She has a long career ahead and is hopeful about its possibilities. Like other district leaders, Manali has had frequent interaction with the state leadership, which is the third rung of the governance structure.

The state leadership consists of the **key party strategists** for respective states. Their role consists of ensuring that district, block and grassroots members have the support that they need (financial or human capital) and that party members are content with their current responsibilities. Parties often prefer that state leaders have strong credibility with district and grassroots leaders. Exceptionally few district leaders are promoted to a state level, and only if they consistently deliver results in their community.

For example, in the Bihar elections of 2016, Rajiv Pratap Rudy was deputed to work in Bihar. Rudy started his political career from Bihar as an MLA. The decision to have him lead the campaign in the state was an intuitive one for the BJP. In regional parties, state leaders have the added responsibility of spending a significant amount of time travelling to meet with various party members.

In early 2014, I met Mukul Roy, state leader for the

Trinamool Congress. Roy looked incredibly fatigued. I asked him if everything was alright. 'Didi (Mamata Banerjee) has given me the responsibility of ensuring that we secure Lok Sabha seats. It is a big responsibility,' he replied, while scrolling through his phone and skimming to see if any important texts had arrived. 'I have been travelling non-stop across districts in North Bengal, spending two days in each place. I haven't seen my family in over a month and I fear that my blood sugar maybe acting up because I have been eating whatever the party members offer,' he added.

Mukul Roy was one of three state leaders who were following a punishing schedule. He would sit through countless meetings that ran for fourteen hours a day, listening to district leaders and party members. After completing their travels in each district, he would call Mamata Banerjee and inform her about how the workers were doing in each district. The life of state leaders is stressful. The state leadership reports to the high command.

The party 'high command' is a phrase borrowed from Congress party jargon, and is the highest-ranking body of individuals in parties. Most political parties have a small group of leaders who jointly make decisions. These are the movers and shakers in the party and every political aspirant hopes to be noticed by them. If you are lucky enough to be noted by the senior leadership, then your career is likely to get a bump up.

For example, in Narendra Modi's early years in the BJP, L.K. Advani took notice of his organizational capacity, nudging party leadership to involve Modi in key programmes such as organising rallies and *pad yatra*s (marches). This helped push Modi into the limelight.

Increasingly, though, an individual rather than a body of people runs the high command. For example, in All India Anna

Dravida Munnetta Kazhagam (AIADMK), it was rumoured that it was mandatory for MPs to carry a photograph of Jayalalitha, a.k.a., 'Amma' in their breast pockets, as a reminder of their allegiance to her. Until her death in late 2016, a strict rule was implicit that Amma, being the ultimate decision maker, could not be questioned.

The high command has an additional responsibility in in national parties. As you will notice in the diagram, the high command oversees the strategic arm or business development unit. These people are responsible for building the party's national brand, the ones you see or hear about most frequently. For example, the national spokesperson on the nine o'clock news on most news channels is a part of the communication team of a national party that is responsible for ensuring that the party's national message is widely circulated.

Similarly, fundraisers for the party are also considered strategically relevant as they bring in resources for the party to contest elections. It is rumoured, though there is very little information about them, that they are the people behind-the-scene with strong connections to industries. The strategic arm within political parties often consists of people who have demonstrated exceptional capabilities through their work, and those have close ties with the party high command. In chapters to follow, you will come to see how money is the Achilles' heel of politics.

One example we can take note of is Priyanka Chaturvedi, the spokesperson for the Congress. Chaturvedi had joined the Congress youth wing and was an active member. However, she was made the spokesperson when she was able to showcase her 1,50,000 followers on Twitter. The INC needed young people with social media presence and she fit the bill.

The diagram simplifies an understanding of the party

structure and has been created after having had several conversations with senior leadership. Oftentimes, there are overlaps between roles and responsibilities, and depending on context, some version of the diagram above is adopted. Unfortunately, most parties shy away from drawing out such explicit structures and most functioning still happens through verbal communication.

My intent in sharing the diagram with you is to ask you to be mindful of the general outlay that tends to exist in party structures, and to identify where and how you can enter into parties. If you want to grow within a party, it is important that you understand how it functions.

How Do You Get Noticed?

You can rise within a party by proving your merit. Every party's leadership makes a conscious effort to take note of upcoming leaders and despite several conversations on the rise of dynastic politicians, most of our leaders have risen through merit. However, parties look for a very specific kind of skill set in promoting individuals. It is important to have some of these to come into the limelight as a promising leader:

Organizational skills, i.e., the capacity to bring together the masses: Political parties hold many rallies, public meetings, protests and other events that require masses to congregate. Policies and ideological stances are announced at these events. Most of us have watched leaders on television share their thoughts and insights while thousands listen patiently. Indian democratic political history is rooted in such events. Party leadership measures the party's popularity by the number of people who attend these rallies. Party workers are asked to bring in people, leveraging their social capital to invite community members to attend. Party members cover the costs of transporting people to such events, and on some occasions even provide food and/or money as incentives for attendance. If party members do well when asked to organize such events, they might even be rewarded with the opportunity to speak at public meetings, consequently drawing notice. A promising way to build a strong rapport is to establish your capacity to bring masses together to attend rallies, protests and events. Senior party leadership will certainly take note of this.

Lalu Prasad Yadav was a phenomenal organizer. Several journalists strongly voice that he has had the gift of gab and the ability to build relationships from a very young age. His brothers have narrated stories of how he had the attention of all young girls in town by putting on a show every day. This singing and dancing transformed into talent for witty speech on stage. As a leader in the Patna Students' Union, he honed his network and built loyal followers who always turned up to hear him speak. Lalu was jailed along with hordes of young men and women during the Emergency. Later, he consciously built his social capital over the years, using his wit, humour, and capacity for articulation,to go on to become a recognized leader in Bihar. Politicians often refer to such qualities as 'mass appeal.'

Election Strategy, i.e., the ability to win elections: Elections are defining moments for political parties. It is during this time that parties most actively seek high performers who can help them win. Most political aspirants join various parties during elections because they realize that work will be most advantageous during election season. One example of this is Kanishka Singh, who quit his high-paying private sector job to join the Sheila Dixit campaign, and was to work extensively in the Delhi state election. He came in to Rahul Gandhi's notice during this time and went on to become one of Rahul Gandhi's closest aides.

Your capacity to demonstrate that you can help win elections can make you infinitely valuable to senior leadership. How you contribute to this process can vary. Big businesses end up funding political campaigns to get in the party's good graces, and community influencers end up bringing in voters. However, my recommendation would be that you use your intellect and academic background for this process.

Take a look at the career of Prashant Kishor, a qualified public health expert who gained experience of polling and data collection during his work with international health agencies. Kishor came in to Modi's circle for his insights on public health. It was during the Gujarat elections of 2012 that Kishor was able to successfully convert his knowledge of health policy towards politics. He rose to national prominence in the general election of 2014 where he supported BJP in its election campaign as political advisor. He was a data genius who used this ability to read sentiments on the ground. He has started a notable youth support group, the Citizens for Accountable Governance. In helping senior political leaders during elections, most recently Nitish Kumar, he is able to garner their support and trust.

Fundraising, i.e., financial support for parties: Parties look for funds to support their operations and candidates and so any individual who can provide a sizeable donation is valued. Unfortunately, as most of us do not have that kind of disposable income, we cannot receive the attention of political parties this way. But the power corridors of Delhi do speak of people who 'buy their way' in to tickets to the Rajya Sabha and Lok Sabha.

In the December 2016 session of parliament, there were rumours that certain business leaders had bought their way into the Rajya Sabha, with each candidate being charged a little over ten crores for this prized seat. Several candidates had invested their personal funds to find their way into parliament, also having brought with them other party donors. Financials are important for a party. However, policies on how parties can be governed make it very hard for a potential candidate to transparently donate to a party and subsequently become a parliamentarian. Thus, unless very necessary, it might not be the best channel of entry.

Networks, or garnering support from the right people: Most of us assume that the only possibility for networking in politics is if you come from a political family, and therefore dismiss the use of our networks. This is not entirely true. Politics is about people, and your ability to build friendships and trust with senior party leaders is critical for the process.

A senior party leader once shared with me that he had helped a young man rise through the political ranks because 'he *looked* sincere and committed.' Their friendship began when the young man had offered to help pen the leader's autobiography. 'This young man had told me that he would help me write a book. I am not a writer but I was touched that he thought I had enough stories to share,' the veteran politician confessed. The project prompted a life-long friendship where the leader became a mentor to the younger politician, opening many doors for the young man who eventually became a cabinet minister.

Beneath the ability to network is the capacity of one to build trust and loyalty, which are two of the most valuable tools in politics. Who do you stand by? How do you support them in their time of need? Do you have unquestionable loyalty to the party and the individual? These are incredibly important in politics. It is why those leaders without concrete skill sets are given key leadership positions when parties are formed. Loyalty and trust are critical in politics.

Rising within a political party is one thing, but getting a ticket to contest for elections is another. If you gain enough prominence within a political party, you are likely to get a ticket from a constituency to contest for election. In the next section, I hope to share a bit more about how politicians get a party ticket.

How Does a Candidate Get a Ticket?

Ask any politician, and they will tell you that candidates are selected by a joint decision in the senior leadership. If you ask them about the factors that come into play, they will tell you that 'winnability' is prime. The process of ticket distribution is a black hole. Most politicians often find themselves fretting right before candidate lists are released, unsure if they will have made the cut. Even the most seasoned politicians are insecure of their chances at having their term renewed and of getting further chances from the party leadership. This insecurity often drives politicians to work constantly to maintain strong relationships within the party.

After several discussions, I have been able to put together some insights on the way in which political parties select candidates, and the main criteria they consider as important for winning an election. Before you even think about being considered for a ticket, it is important that you establish yourself as someone who can bring tangible value to the party: this will put you on the shortlist for candidates. The decision to get a ticket typically comes from party leadership. In regional parties this is often one person at the top, while in national parties it is a collective group of people.

An informal set of metrics do exist to evaluate if a party is fit to contest elections and likely to win. Party leaders(s) often consult with a set of confidantes to evaluate candidates. The criteria list is as follows:

What makes a candidate winnable? Taking the party's view

Criteria	What does it mean?	Who are the exceptions?	Weightage
Caste/community of candidate	Identity politics around caste and religion continue to play a major role in Indian politics. It is important that most candidates bring a certain background to politics.	Not all states maintain the same dynamics around identity. States like West Bengal are not big on caste equations but are on religious issues. Identity implies trust, and those who are not from the same caste/religion but bring in sufficient trust are considered valuable.	Very relevant

Criteria	What does it mean?	Who are the exceptions?	Weightage
Ability to mobilize people	You must have the capacity to mobilize people for campaigning: whether people you know in the community, through your eloquent speeches, or with resources to gain people's attention to vote for you.	Mobilizing people is key to politics and there can be no exceptions.	Very relevant
Relationship with party workers	Party workers are the foot soldiers of elections who go in to the community and garner votes for you. Parties take the relationship that you have with party workers into consideration before giving you a ticket. A strong following within the party worker base has a significant advantage.	There are many cases where even without a strong relationship with party workers, individuals are offered tickets for bringing in something more valuable to the party.	Somewhat relevant

Criteria	What does it mean?	Who are the exceptions?	Weightage
Funding capacity	Increasingly, money is playing an important role in politics. Those who can fund their own campaign and are less of a financial burden on the party are appreciated. A candidate's capacity to fund and support his own political campaign is now an asset.	Funding, though gaining importance, cannot trump other qualities. Established national parties have a number of professionals willing to fund their own campaign, but don't give them tickets since they are lacking other qualities.	Somewhat relevant
Standing within the community	As discussions about crime and politics becomes prominent, political parties realize that it is important to gauge the standing of an individual within the community. Some questions raised now are:	Despite party efforts to gauge the 'standing of a candidate' in a community, many criminals still contest and win elections. As you can see, your standing within the community is still not a primary factor.	Somewhat relevant

Criteria	What does it mean?	Who are the exceptions?	Weightage
	Does s/he have criminal records? Is s/he perceived to be ethical? Some parties now do a background check in the community before giving out tickets.		
Ability to contribute to the party in the future	Pollsters, political strategists and fundraisers are few of the many 'new-age' professionals who have entered politics, offering new skill sets that can help parties grow. Political parties are not just looking at your winnability in elections today, but also what you can offer them in the future. It is important for professionals to identify what they can contribute to the party's future.	This is still relatively new thinking within parties. While some individuals have been able to convey their value addition, others are working towards it.	Somewhat relevant

There is often very little discourse within parties about why certain people are favoured over others for tickets to contest elections. This lack of discourse is interesting given that it is a tremendously subjective method that is employed. What little knowledge you have of the factors that help the selection of candidates, however, should assist in your preparation as an aspiring politician.

Reflecting on the Present State

Most politicians learn about the party by being in the system. But before you join the party system, some idea of the motivations, structures and functioning of Indian political party systems is useful. Joining and working within a political party is a major ideological and personal commitment, so it is important that before you join, you ask yourself a few things.

Questions to ask yourself	Answers
Do I understand the implications of joining party X?	
What does the party aim to do?	
What is party X's vision of strong governance?	
Where do I see myself fitting into this political party's system?	
What do I have to offer to the party?	
Why will the party value my presence?	

Questions to ask yourself	Answers
What can I learn from this party?	
How do I want to rise within this political party?	
What is my path for doing so?	
What is my end goal in joining this party?	

SECTION II
Ensuring Professional Growth

SECTION II
Ensuring Professional Growth

Chapter 4

How Do You Prepare for Politics Professionally?

Politics is the profession of mobilizing people in support of a common cause. Successful politicians have in their previous professions learnt and practiced skills relating to winning the hearts and minds of voters. Whether you are a youth leader who has a tremendous following and an understanding of what people need, or a corporate professional with acumen to poll public opinion and assess people's requirements, you must begin by **identifying** and **honing** politically valuable skills that you possess. No one profession can completely prepare you for a career in politics, but your profession and/or educational background can offer you elements that are relevant to politics. As you think of transitioning into politics full time, ask yourself whether:

- Your existing job or position is able to provide you with the skill set that will benefit your political career.
- How you will add more skills through your current job, new activities, or transition to a new position that will make you a successful politician.

What possible deficits exist in your current skill set that you can make up for, and how.

Reading this chapter will not be enough. Your 'To do' should include evaluating:

- What are my skill sets and how do they relate to a political career?
- What do I need to do to build on them so that I can be a value addition for the mobilization of votes?
- What are the new skills I can acquire by learning and/or working in the constituency?

Create a timeline for building your core skill set.

Looking Back...

In 1885, the Scotsman Octavian Hume decided to convene a group of intellectuals, professionals and academics to discuss issues affecting Indians in the Empire. This brought together a group of foreign educated barristers, with Womesh Chandra Banerjee acting as first president, to form the Indian National Congress (INC). The space for conversations in this group soon transformed: Indians began to evolve demands on how they expected to be governed. At first, the intellectuals in the group were not representative of the restless majority suffering at the hands of the British. The INC expanded and began to include members from all walks of life. The party valued people who could bring in others to support their cause.

From Bal Gangadhar Tilak, who had deep-rooted connections to the community through public service, to Matangini Hazra whose defiance of the British rule became an inspiration for others to join the Indian independence movement, politics has always sought people who have the **personality, resources** and/or **intellect** to draw people to their ideology and vision. Sardar Vallabhbhai Patel was one of a new generation of leaders of the Indian independence movement who stood out in his ability to garner people's support.

Vallabhbhai Patel was the son of Zaverbhai, born in 1875. He showed signs of leadership from a young age when he refused to take unjust orders from teachers or tolerate their failures in performing their responsibilities. When he was eighteen, he staged a protest, picketing a teacher who bullied a student. He often won these battles and his enthusiasm to serve the public grew through his school years.

The classroom was not able to contain his zeal for action. He took his first plunge into politics by running a grassroots campaign for an old teacher with minimal resources whose political opponent was a wealthy businessman. He mobilized votes that finally won his teacher the election. Eventually, Vallabhbhai Patel became a lawyer and practiced law for several years. By May 1917, when he saw that the Ahmedabad Municipality was in a dismal economic condition under a dictatorial administrative head, he swooped in to win the election and pushed out a tyrannical administrator. He was a successful in fixing systems as a municipal commissioner.

Vallabhbhai Patel always used his **intellect** to understand people, working to improve their trust in him by better interaction. As a municipal commissioner, he learned how to be **resourceful** in working within the system to serve the people.

Vallabhbhai Patel's skills were to be tested to their limit when he first worked closely with Mahatma Gandhi in a non-violent protest in Nadid, Gujarat. He worked as Gandhi's deputy.

Farmer's crops were failing in Nadid, and Vallabhbhai Patel called for the British to relax taxes that year. But the British administration did not relent. Gandhi and Patel decided to hold a Satyagraha. The two of them travelled together across sixty villages to convince farmers to sign a petition against the government's oppressive taxation regime. The British government pushed back, auctioning off land of those farmers who defaulted. Patel consoled the community and told them not to be intimidated. When Gandhi had to leave, Patel took charge in Nadid and continued to travel to different villages to motivate farmers to stay strong. After four months of tension, the British government gave in to the demands and taxes were relaxed.

The movement was the first of many protests for Vallabhbhai Patel, who soon came to be known as Sardar. Sardar Vallabhbhai Patel became an established face in the independence movement and a close confidante of Mahatma Gandhi.[3]

'Political parties have always sought people who have personality, resources and/or intellect.'

What does that mean?

- Personality: in the lead up to the general elections of 2014, Mamata Banerjee decided to give Dev, a Bengali film super-star, the ticket to contest. Party members were dismayed because he was not a career politician but Mamata stuck to her decision. He not only won the parliamentary seat by a landslide victory, but continues to draw lakhs of voters to every rally he attends. 'Personality' is the ability to leverage an individual's existing brand in support of a party. Movie stars, athletes, and internationally recognized professionals fall in this cohort.

[3] Balraj, Krishna, *India's Bismarck, Sardar Vallabhbhai Patel*, Mumbai: Indus Source Books, 2007.

- Resources: Madhu Goud's successful law firm had made him financially sound but not spiritually happy. He decided to leave his law firm and come to India to contest the Lok Sabha election. A Union Minister and a senior Congress leader also sought the seat he was after. But when Madhu Goud made it known that he would fund his own election, the party willingly gave him the seat. Goud went on to contest and win the election. 'Resources' are the ability – as an independent candidate, party fundraiser or party donor – that would ultimately strengthen the party base. Wealthy and independent business personas offer the same.
- Intellect: Jairam Ramesh first got in to Indian politics as the 'back office' strategist to the Congress party, conducting policy and electoral research for the party. After years of providing his electoral and political acumen, he finally came into parliament. 'Intellect' is the capacity to use political intelligence to benefit the party. This is the most frequently used path for educated and accomplished professionals. However, what you offer to party leaders must be politically relevant.

Patel's career as municipal commissioner, preceding his decision to join Mahatma Gandhi, had given him hands-on experience of how to mobilize people. He took it upon himself to serve people at a local level even in pre-Independence India, and then worked his way up through to the national level. He had managed, campaigned and organized large scale protests.

The people, stories and qualities of the Indian independence movement have framed our current political discourse.

To examine how politicians acquire their skill sets, let us look at careers pursued by parliamentarians before they joined office. Below is a pie chart that breaks down professions pursued by parliamentarians before they entered politics.

Comparing Parliamentarians Professions

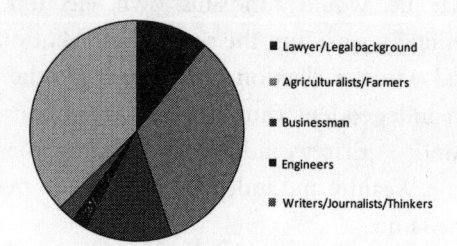

- Lawyer/Legal background
- Agriculturalists/Farmers
- Businessman
- Engineers
- Writers/Journalists/Thinkers

Careers in the First Parliament

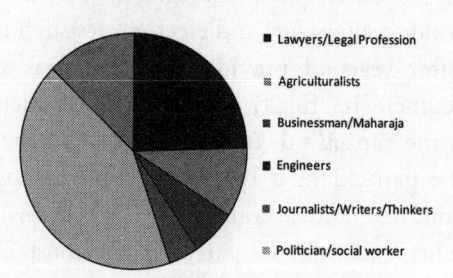

- Lawyers/Legal Profession
- Agriculturalists
- Businessman/Maharaja
- Engineers
- Journalists/Writers/Thinkers
- Politician/social worker

Careers in the Fifteenth Parliament

The chart above makes it evident that politics attracts some careers more than others. Consider, for example, that in our first and fifteenth Lok Sabha, lawyers and career politicians make up more than half the elected representatives in the house. Business leaders have taken up the space of maharajas. Journalists and writers also have a notable presence in the parliament. Specific careers offer skills more amenable for a career in politics. For example, business leaders have extensive experience in managing events and people and make for strong political leaders. In the upcoming sections, we try to dissect why certain professions and life experiences can make you a good political leader.

Identifying the Relevance of Your Career to Politics

Identify Ideology	Convince voters that you can deliver said promise	Get votes so that you can deliver on manifesto
• Ability to find the pulse of the priorities of people • Convert priorities to electoral promises that resonate with people • Ensure that channels of communication during elections are sound	• Bring in community leaders and champions who can endorse statement • Reach out to all pertinent demographics which could vote for the respective party • Be able to convince voters about the merit of the promise	• Get the voters to the closest voting booth on polling day • Monitor and ensure that election rules are followed and candidates are not disqualified • Make a last push for the candidates in the lead up to the election

A successfully elected parliamentarian's job is deceptively straightforward: s/he must identify a promise that resonates with voters and convince them why s/he is the most fit to deliver that promise, and secure the vote to win the election. But the electoral process is more complex than that. For example, the promise the candidate hopes to deliver might not be the right promise. A candidate needs to tap into the pulse of the people to understand what is important to them.

Political pundits argue that in the general elections of 2014, Narendra Modi was able to assess that Indians had become more aspirational. He also knew that Indians were not completely about development. There was an underbelly of identity politics as well. Throughout his campaign trail, Modi blended his rhetoric to speak of jobs and development but also community and religion. His special blend in speeches hit the nerve of the voter and people wanted to give him a chance. The result was that Modi fared better than Rahul Gandhi with his speeches on subsidies and handouts.

When convincing voters that you are the person most fit to deliver on a promise, your reputation within the community and affiliations to political parties matters significantly. For example, during the Odisha Panchayat elections in 2017, several rookie candidates from BJP won seats, beating the established BJD that had been in power for over three decades. When pollsters tried to figure out why they had elected these people, voters reported that they believed in the profile and background of the local candidates and thought that with the BJP at centre, candidates would have a much better chance at delivering development promises. 'We can sense whether the candidate will work for us on the basis of who is supporting them within the community and at a state level,' one voter shared. The BJP had been stellar in ensuring that voters were in the know of the strengths of each candidate, and that they could back these candidates in their work.

Getting votes in your favour often requires ensuring that the voter remains convinced of your stance enough to end up at the polling booth to cast their vote in your support. In the general elections of 2014, the Citizens for Accountable Governance (CAG), an outfit of the BJP that was staffed by young professionals from top firms like Boston Consulting Group and Tata Consultancy Services was created to equip key constituencies with people who would ensure that voters remained convinced of the BJP platform. The CAG team orchestrated a series of communication campaigns that highlighted Narendra Modi's development agenda, including the hologram-based speeches and tea-time with Modi ('Chai pe Charcha') across the country. The innovative use of technology showed the voter how Modi was a forward thinker, and also strengthened the BJP brand. They managed to keep the attention of the voter enough to bring them to the voting booth.

As you would have gauged by now, entering politics requires a host of skills and a gamut of tasks. Being able to study, practice and prepare for these tasks will make you a strong electoral candidate. Some of these skill sets are acquired through formal education, but most can be learned through the work place or in any professional environment. Earlier we saw how certain professions provide exposure to necessary skills in politics to parliamentarians. Accordingly, we will discuss six most common professions that parliamentarians pursue, and dissect the skills these professions offer. Be sure to recognize these skills and practice them through the route suggested below.

- Youth politics
- Legal practice
- Social work
- Bureaucratic work
- Advisory positions
- Celebrity status

Youth Politics

Some of the political wings for youth politics in India are the Indian Youth Congress (IYC), Akhil Bharatiya Vidhyarti Parishad (ABVP), National Students Unions of India (NSUI) and Students Federation of India (SFI). Youth wings are an opportunity for political parties to indoctrinate young minds with party ideology and recruit promising talent directly in to the party. Youth party workers are also recruited as volunteers during election campaigns, giving young leaders exposure to the electoral process and helping them build social capital with leaders. Youth politics serves a training ground for many politicians.

Take, for example, Nupur Sharma, the young candidate who stood against Arvind Kejriwal in the Delhi elections of 2015. Sharma acknowledges her decision to join ABVP as a turning point in her career. Without a family history in politics, it was a fresh experience. Mentored by senior college leaders, Sharma was exposed to thinking about student policies, relating to her peers, and even campaign for some of her classmates. She eventually ran for ABVP office that gave her first hand exposure. Sharma says that being able to work actively on the ground for the party brought her to the notice of senior BJP leaders like Arun Jaitley. 'I was working long days and was completely devoted to ABVP. I had run campaigns and held positions within the ABVP … in the BJP, when you do strong grassroots work, senior leaders acknowledge you for it.' After several years in ABVP leadership, Sharma's contribution was duly noted and she was offered an election ticket to contest for chief minister of Delhi. Though Sharma lost that election, her future is bright since she is recognized by senior party leaders and has the experience and social capital to grow.

Benefits of being in youth politics:
- Early learning about the political system and realities on the ground
- Exposure to the electoral process
- Hands-on training on connecting with and mobilizing communities
- Building networks and connections from early on with other politicos

It is not a coincidence that members in Narendra Modi's cabinet are from student movements. Political parties like the BJP and CPI(M) have meritocratic preferences and recruit dedicated party workers who are well-known within the network. Since youth wings demonstrate commitment from early on in a career, they are a good pool for recruitment. Being involved in youth politics allows you to intimately understand the people and the workings within the system. However, if you are interested in youth politics you must be mindful that it is very likely to hamper your academic performance.

A significant downside to youth politics is that most of the politicking happens on campus, and often at the cost of one's education. Political parties require significant time and attention of young leaders, and this puts education on the back burner. You are likely to be expected to skip a class to attend a protest, or might be arrested when picketing for a cause (most youth leaders have been arrested at least once).

But a young mind should invest in learning as much as possible before joining the electoral process. So while youth politics might establish reputation at an early age as a political leader, it is important to note that it comes at the high cost of losing education.

Lawyers

Some of the successful lawyers who have thrived in national politics are Kapil Sibal, Arun Jaitley, P. Chidambaran, Meenakshi Lekhi and Manish Tewari. With their exhaustive knowledge of the intricacies of governance, they are able to prepare for political careers effectively. As we have already seen, the first Indian National Congress was filled with lawyers educated abroad. Today, lawyers also play a very practical role for most political parties.

There are instances where senior political leaders or national political parties have been summoned by the judiciary in court cases. Some examples include the case against Kanhaiya Kumar for sedition, the case with the Association for Democratic Reforms (ADR) versus the Union of India, the National Herald scam, and the accusation against Augusta Westland. In each of these cases, senior political leaders who are lawyers (and often MPs) represent political leaders or parties in court. Lawyers, with their extensive knowledge and ability to represent political parties in court, are a valuable asset, especially given the number of lawsuits against political parties.

A lawyer once told me that he had been elected to the Rajya Sabha having won the murder case against Shibhu Soren . 'After the case was over, he [Shibhu Soren] patted me on the back and said, "I am very happy today and I owe you a great deal. I want to make you a Rajya Sabha MP. What do you think?" I was taken aback but then thought to myself that I have saved this guy from years in prison. So when the Rajya Sabha seat opened up and he said he wanted to gift it to me, I gladly accepted,' the MP told me with pride.

Aspiring politicians also use the court to come into the good graces of the public. For example, Meenakashi Lekhi first entered public service by providing pro bono legal services to poor women. She often talks of how she took notice of women in need and fought for their rights as their lawyer. This work gave her credibility within the community.

Benefits of being a lawyer:
- Detailed understanding of governance systems
- Opportunity to provide valuable support to the political class
- Opportunity to provide professional services to people in need

But it is possible to study governance structures without being a lawyer. Dinesh Trivedi was first thrust into the political sphere when he filed and won a Public Interest Litigation (PIL) to protect consumer interests. 'I wanted to help the people,' he declared. 'I had to study hard and long to understand the contours of the law, but I wanted to serve the public and was passionate about the cause,' he explained. But be warned: the judicial system in India is even more complicated than the legislature, and you must invest time to understand its complexities.

Social Worker

Political aspirants who come from a background of social work maintain an exhaustive knowledge and understanding of their community's needs and sentiments. Many political aspirants choose to spend a few years deeply embedded in their constituency prior to contesting elections. This is also an opportunity to gain trust and social capital, in addition to understanding their expectations. This goes a long way in politics, as parties often give tickets to candidates who are well-connected to communities.

Dr Manda Jagannath, a four-time parliamentarian from Andhra Pradesh, first came to the notice of T.N. Rama Rao and Chandra Babu Naidu for his strong connection to the scheduled caste community in Nagarkurnool. 'I wanted our people to have better education and public services and I began by working to understand why that hasn't happened yet,' he said. Jagannath used to visit the houses of community members and listen to their hopes, aspirations and dreams. He spent his student life building relationships with the community, and was present by their side on every occasion. On graduating from medical school, he went on to hold medical camps for community members. 'In those days you didn't have as much access to healthcare, and even the simplest of health camps could make a remarkable difference for poor people,' he explained. 'My weekends were spent serving people of my community.'

As Jagannath got more involved in his community, he began to be increasingly vocal about putting in place basic systems and rights for the scheduled castes. Even though his daytime job was as a professor at Osmania University, he dedicated the remainder of his time to being a social worker, representing the concerns of his community in various political platforms. His strong hold in the community led the Telugu Desam Party (TDP) to offer him a ticket that marked the start of his national electoral career.

An interesting facet of Jagannath's career was that his contact with the political class as a social worker. He attended party rallies and met with local leaders, building relationships with political heavy weights within his community. He recognized that social work alone would not help him get a party ticket and that he needed to be in the political circuit for this. This combination kept him in the political light.

Benefits of being a social worker:
- Connection to the community
- Recognition of your work by the party
- Endorsement of community leaders
- Ability to get a pulse of the requirements and possible electoral promises from the community

The AAP gave Medha Patkar a ticket to contest from Mumbai in the general elections of 2014. Patkar is a terrific organizer who can connect with communities to effectively mobilize them in support of a specific cause, quite similar to a politician in this regard. She is also a recognisable name. But Patkar lost the election because she lacked a key quality seen in politicians. 'The political machinery is built around a leader having the capacity to work through party workers to bring in the vote. You cannot just know the community, you also need to know your party workers. That is why it is not enough to be a social worker. You have to have the capacity to work with local party workers to turn those connections into votes. Patkar didn't have that,' explained Jayant Ghoshal, a senior journalist.

In considering your political career, it is important that you make social work a core part of your trajectory. You have to know your constituency and its requirements. This must be closely complemented with your connection to local party workers.

Bureaucrat

The bureaucracy is the lifeline of the governance machinery in India. Bureaucrats as executors and administrators make the government move. Even though only select bureaucrats are required to interface with politicians, most maintain a relationship with local political leaders as part of the scope of their work. For example, a District Magistrate is likely to receive multiple requests from their respective on the implementation of development projects in her/his constituency and the timely allocations of Local Area Development Funds.

Bureaucrats from the Indian Administrative Services (IAS) and Indian Police Services (IPS) are the most likely to be connected with the political class. This space is optimal for political aspirants, by providing the opportunity to serve constituents as part of the job while also having relationships with political leaders. You will notice that there are several retired civil servants in politics.

One phenomenal civil servant who became a politician is Dr Ajoy Kumar from Jamshedpur. 'I was posted in Bihar for only three months. But when I was leaving, there was a twelve kilometre human chain along the rail line to see me off,' explained Kumar about his first stint in the IPS. His illustrious career in in the IPS brought him several accolades, including an award for bravery for his involvement in a twelve-hour shoot out with dangerous dacoits.

Dr Kumar was transferred to Jamshedpur at the request of the Tatas, and it was a turning point in his career.

On his first day at work, he heard that a local political leader had shot his neighbour in broad daylight. When he went to arrest the leader, he was threatened by a call from a senior political leader. He answered the call with confidence: 'Sir, if you don't want justice to be served here, I will leave, but if I have proof that the person has committed murder, I do not want you to interfere. I will put him behind bars.' The leader backed down. He disconnected the phone and never called in a 'favour' again. 'No one could leave the house after dark,' Kumar explained. 'But within three months we had created an environment where people were out of their houses till two or three in the morning,' he told me with pride.

Kumar's reputation as a police officer led Babulal Marandi, the then chief minister of Jharkhand to ask him to join the newly formed Jharkhand Vikas Morcha (JVM) to contest from Jamshedpur for the parliament seat. Dr Kumar won the election. Though Kumar had always maintained political ambitions, it was his service as a police officer that helped him transition into a successful politician. He is currently the National Spokesperson for the INC.

Others like Harish Chandra Meena, a senior officer from the IPS, and Nand Kishore Singh, a senior officer from the IAS, have also transitioned to become successful parliamentarians. Like lawyers, their thorough knowledge of systems of governance is a tremendous asset.

Benefits of being a bureaucrat:
- Direct connect to the community as a public servant.
- Strong opportunity to connect with the political class.
- Detailed knowledge of government systems and cultures.

But the structure of the bureaucracy in India seems to be changing quickly. There is a wave of lateral appointments entering the bureaucracy in the form of fellows, interns or consultants. Young professionals have a new opportunity to make an impact on the ground and win credibility with communities and local leaders in a new avatar. Fellowships and programmes are just beginning to be rolled out, but they hold tremendous promise. You must consider applying for fellowships offered by the state government given the powerful impact it can have on your career.

Advisory Roles

Political parties often require economists, mathematicians, political scientists and other qualified professionals to help them during elections. They look to find professionals who can help strengthen party structures and institutions as a way to garner votes. For example, an economist can help parties in understanding current economic conditions, a mathematician can help them design an opinion poll, and a political scientist can decipher issues within local party units. While there is space for experts and 'thought' leaders, you will need to be able to correlate your knowledge to insights within the political domain.

Experts who make it as successful politicians often work on specific issues with party leaders. Take for example Jay Panda, an MP from Odisha. Panda ran a family business before his entry into politics. His first connection with the political class came when he was bringing together industry leaders to develop insights about the business world. Using his networks, he was able to reach Naveen Patnaik, the son of the chief minister of Odisha at the time, who was thinking of launching his own party. Panda won his confidence by sharing insights about business policies. Eventually, as the elections came up, Panda decided to help Patnaik strategize for his campaign, working in the back office as an intellectual source. Naveen Patnaik won the election to become chief minister, and won his seat in parliament.

Panda used his acumen as a business leader to run a successful campaign. Most intellectuals bring the ability to think critically to the table, which is of tremendous value to politicians. Their skill sets win the attention and trust of political leaders and help them become advisors to politicians. Any background, whether the arts or sciences, can bring value to advisory roles in politics. You have to be able to figure out skill sets for yourself and prepare accordingly.

Benefits of being in an advisory role:
- Appealing to politicians with an in-depth understanding of a field.
- Credibility and background that demands the attention of politicians.
- Analytical strategies on how to win elections.

People without any political background have often made significant headway as advisors to political leadership. Consider Raghav Chandra, a volunteer who joined the AAP while taking a break from studying for Chartered Accountancy exams. Though fresh out of college and in his early twenties, he used his talent and expertise to become a key part of the team. He was an early member of the AAP and helped frame several of its outreach campaigns that were hugely successful during elections. His passion became quickly visible to Arvind Kejriwal, and soon enough, he became the party spokesperson. He was a fierce advocate of the AAP on news channels during the election cycles, and although he did not contest for elections, he became a prominent leader within the party. He was made advisor to the government when AAP came into office. Advisors have to have the capacity to learn quickly and turn their insights to political mileage.

Celebrity Status

'If you want to become a politician in Bengal, you must become a movie star first,' joked a senior leader of the Trinamool Congress (TMC), when party leader Mamata Banerjee decided to dole out tickets to regional film stars, singers and artists. From Hema Malini to Rajyavardhan Singh

Rathore, celebrities have entered into national electoral politics. A celebrity can be an athlete, artist, actor, business leader, or even an international diplomat.

Political parties prefer individuals who have created a name for themselves outside of politics and can bring in something new to the political dimension. In the case of movie stars or athletes, the value proposition is that their existing fan base can be turned into a voter base. For example, a political party will calculate that fans of Shatrughan Sinha, a prominent Hindi film actor, are likely to vote for him in the Bihar elections wherever he goes to campaign and not only his constituency. Similarly, in the case of business leaders, political parties assume that they will bring in their own wealth and mobilize funds from other sources.

One of the most visible celebrities in the current administration is Smriti Irani, who was until recently the minister for Human Resource Development. Irani left her job as an actor in soap operas to join politics. By the time she entered politics, she was a household name. Irani lost her first election in 2009 when she contested on a parliamentary ticket against Kapil Sibal. Her celebrity status did not prove to be of much help in bringing in votes. But her celebrity status proved to be of use when she became a fierce advocate of the BJP on prime time news, especially when she took on the most difficult of anchors. She was quickly called to even the most prominent nine o'clock show and was an articulate speaker. Soon enough, she was given a Rajya Sabha seat and has served two roles in the Cabinet. She was already a household name as a celebrity and now her ability to advocate for BJP on national television was an icing on the cake.

Benefits of being a celebrity:
- An immediate buy-in from political parties.

Political parties are increasingly diversifying their definition of a celebrity. Rather than looking at only those who have been on television or films, political parties are now considering anyone with a brand as a celebrity. For example Shashi Tharoor was a known diplomat who gained international repute when he was nominated to be secretary general. Thus, when he expressed interest to join Indian politics, his celebrity status in the diplomatic circle led him to gain quick repute in politics as well. Political parties are also increasingly open-minded about who they accept. It is possible that you can achieve celebrity status in a field other than cinema and sports to enter into politics.

Those left out...

The list above does not capture all fields and skill sets. The section intends for you to think critically about your skills and identify where you can build them further. This might help you direct your merits and talents to rise up in politics.

The section above also leaves out a large interest group, namely aspiring politicians such as:
- People with a family background in politics.
- Mobs/goons who enter politics to add to their power.

However, as this book does not target readers from political families, nor promote violence or intimidation as a valid political skill set, there is no further discussion of the uses of either. Please note that both these elements are strongly present in the current political scenario, and that you will come across them as an aspiring politician.

Reflecting on the Current Scenario

It is important that you take a step back as you think about your way forward in politics, and understand where you are now and your current skills. Evaluate them and think of what you need to build upon. Below is a table with some sample skills. Run down the list and check how many skills you have, and identify the gaps.

Description of Skill	Do I have it? (Yes/No)	If not, how will you build it? Add a timeline.
Deep understanding of concerns of community and constituency I hope to root myself in:		
Ability to convince people of vision for the community:		
Capacity to articulate my ideas to a large group of people:		
Detailed understanding of how the political party system works:		

Chapter 5

How to Build Your Brand and Message?

A politician's job is to inspire people with their ideas, convince voters and political leaders about policy measures and successfully introduce new programmes to all stakeholders. Politicians master the art of communication in an effort to do their job effectively. From motivating party workers to articulating a party position, politicians are expected to be thinkers, speakers and writers pushing for the greater social good. As an aspiring politician, it is important that you build your communication skills by asking yourself:

- What are the core beliefs and principles that will define my leadership and communication?
- How do I want to communicate these in a way that resonates with my target demographic?
- What is the best method of communication for these in the age of digital media?

Reading this chapter will not be enough. Your 'To do' should include making notes from speeches by world leaders as well as:

- Evaluating your body language as you communicate.
- Learning to exude confidence in your body language.
- Considering principles important to you, to embody in every speech.

Put in place a clear vision of the kind of communicator you want to become.

Looking Back...

E.V. Ramaswamy was born in to a wealthy merchant family in Tamil Nadu in 1879. He was a fierce orator famous for debate, even though he was not known for his academic orientation. He was gregarious as a young man, pulling together joyous social gatherings. His life took a drastic turn in his early twenties when his wife and him lost their child. He left home, depressed.

For several months, Ramaswamy wandered across India. Without any resources or networks of support, he had become homeless and relied on the goodwill of others. He later recounted one instance of a woman selling her body for food to a Brahmin priest, an incident that left a deep impression on him, leaving him disgusted at the hypocrisy of society. These experiences away from home shaped his core principles. He returned home a changed man.

Ramaswamy decided to commit himself to his work and community. In a short time, he gained a standing in the community for his administrative capacity. The community nudged him to become a municipal councillor on taking note of his capacity to solve problems. Wishing to serve the weakest and most vulnerable sections of society, he joined the INC.

Shortly after entering politics, he noticed had the discrimination against the tribal community of Ezhavas in a neighbouring town called Vaikom. Ezhavas were banned not just from entering temples, but also from using public roads and resources. They were a severely deprived and suffering community.

Enraged by the ill treatment, Ramaswamy organized a protest with party members. The party workers travelled to Vaikom to picket for equal treatment of Ezhavas. The local administration returned the Ezhavas their rights to use public resources and religious sites after the noise created by the protest. This marked the first of many battles that Ramaswamy took on to protect the weak and vulnerable, that made him demonstrate his potential early in his political career.

Although Ramaswamy saw the party machinery as a vehicle to protest injustice, he saw that there was severe discrimination within the INC itself, in favour of Brahmins. He noticed that Brahmins held all key positions within the party. He first believed that perhaps that the power capture of the party would change over time and that reservations for non-Brahmin members would be introduced. An incident in Cheranmadevi changed his perception.

V.V.S. Iyer, a Brahmin leader of the INC, ran a gurukulam in Cheranmadevi, Tamil Nadu. News reached Ramaswamy that non-Brahmin students in the gurukulam were made to sit separately and eat from different utensils. He decided to take action against this discrimination. As the gurukulam was run on donations, some from the INC, Ramaswamy lobbied for the party to cut off their donation. However, the INC did not care much for such actions.

Ramaswamy began to realize at this point that the INC nurturing non-Brahmin members was unlikely to happen. While Ramaswamy managed to convince non-Brahmin members to stop donating to the gurukulam and ensured that V.V.S. Iyer was removed from his position, he failed to bring much change within the INC. This incident prompted Ramaswamy to leave the INC.

This departure marked his rebirth as Periyar, a fierce

political and social advocate for equal rights. He recognized the extent to which Brahmins had been systemically oppressing non-Brahmins and concluded that if India were to progress, it needed a casteless and classless society. In 1925, he started the *Kudi Arasu* (*The Republic*), a periodical that carried pieces about reservations for non-Brahmins to work towards equality in society.

Periyar was a prolific writer, using the periodical to communicate the need for all castes and religious denominations to have equal rights. Periyar began to translate the journal into English in order to reach a different demographic, continuing to advocate equal rights for all communities. He spearheaded the Self-Respect Movement, advocating equal representation in the political sphere.

Peiryar also travelled extensively across Tamil Nadu to spread his message, speaking zealously on equal treatment of all castes, a topic close to his heart. This brought him attention from all over the world. Through his writing and speaking engagements, he was able to communicate his core principles and build a strong brand. Soon, Periyar was invited to speak across Asia and Europe to share his vision for a more equal India.

Though Periyar had left the INC to focus completely on communicating to the world the merits of equality, he continued to be in contact with politicians. Periyar pushed for Tamil leaders to adopt a stronger Dravidian identity. He was tireless in organizing protests to question the government's existing policies. Periyar believed and said that change could be initiated through legislative measures. He used his political capital to bring attention to this issue.

Eventually, Periyar went on to become the father of the Dravidian movement in Tamil Nadu and headed the Dravida

Munnetra Kazhagam (DMK). His speeches and writing became the backbone for the ideology of the DMK and has continued to set the tone of politics in Tamil Nadu.

What is political communication? Who are we targeting?

Political communication is mindful messaging crafted with the intent of persuading voters and/or other politicians. It can be communicated through writing, speeches or even on social media (for example, tweets on Twitter). Political communication is defined by the intent rather than the medium. It typically targets three core stakeholders: voters, party members and the media (who then communicate to others). What follows is an outline of how most politicians communicate with each stakeholder.

Voters: Whether a politician is in the Lok Sabha or Rajya Sabha, s/he is expected to interface with voters. A successful politician can gauge the pulse of the people and speak to them on topics in a language that resonates with them.

The MP Kalikesh Singh Deo learned the value of studying voter behaviour carefully at the young age of nine. In his native town of Bolangir, he accompanied his uncles on the campaign trail. Kalikesh recalls walking nearly 9 kilometres to reach a distant village on the trail, one in particular that had neither electricity nor water.

After the treacherous hike to the village, where the villagers tended to their comfort, Kalkesh's uncles had anticipated that villagers would demand infrastructure and development. But the villagers' response shook them. Unanimously, the villagers asked for a temple. 'How could you ask for a temple when you have nothing here?', blurted one of his uncles. The villagers responded saying, 'Once we have God, everything else will follow.' Although a counter-intuitive response, their emotions were such.

In order to communicate effectively, you need to understand the pulse of the voter. Your assumptions of their priority may not always match. It is important that you develop a message that will resonate strongly with their thinking, by continually staying in touch with their priorities.

Party members: Sometimes politicians need to convince their own party members of the party ideology with strong articulation. From explaining why one deserves to get a ticket to what election strategy will likely win more votes and to how to structure a recruitment drive, a politician spends significant time with her/his own party members. This ability is particularly important when contesting for elections, and I saw this first hand with a TMC candidate during the general elections of 2014.

The candidate in question did not have any roots in the constituency. He was marked as an outsider. He spent a better part of his initial days trying to communicate his confidence in his campaign from that specific constituency, explaining why he thought he had a chance at winning. Despite several attempts, there was continuous fighting within the party. Three factions emerged within the first week: those who supported him, those who did not support him and those who were willing to support him in exchange for money.

The party's central leadership could provide only so much support, consumed as they were with all other candidates. The candidate had to unite the party workers by himself to hold rallies and public meetings. He struggled throughout, constantly finding himself in positions of having to convince party workers of his value. With two weeks to go for the election, he still faced a situation where party members refused to canvas for him because they did not believe he had a chance at winning. Ultimately, he lost the election.

A key part of being a politician is the ability to get people on your side. You have to have the capacity to win people and their trust as well as keep them on your side. This example above shows us how the candidate failed to do so and paid the price.

Media/external communication: In today's context, it is imperative that a politician look beyond the party and the voter and get the message across to a larger audience. A politician today has to have the capacity to communicate through the media as well. It is not surprising that the BJP made it mandatory for ministers to set up handles to use Twitter and communicate with the general public.

In the state elections in Delhi in 2014, both the AAP and BJP recognized that humour and social media were a terrific combination. In fact, they noted that young people log in to social media for their daily dose of humour. Each party set up teams to float jokes about opposition leaders, pushing them to become viral. On any given day, thousands of people would take note of the jokes on Facebook. In today's electronic age, you cannot overlook the role of media.

Periyar established his political legacy by 1. Identifying principles that were most important to him, 2. Communicating his principles and vision for a new India through his writing and speeches, and 3. Working with the political class to push for change. During the turn of the twentieth century, most political leaders mastered the ability to articulate their ideas through speeches and writing. From Mahatma Gandhi to Jawaharlal Nehru to Madan Mohan Malviya, India's founding fathers have effectively communicated their vision for the country using different media.

Inevitably, oral and written communication has extended beyond the individual into the political party. Today, most political parties share their core principles through publications. For example, the INC publishes the *Congress Sandesh* and the BJP publishes the *Kamal Sandesh*, both flagship party publications. Several journalists have often found their way in to the Rajya Sabha and Lok Sabha by advising party leadership on how best to frame messages that would resonate with the public. However, political parties now look beyond print to spread their message.

In an age where WhatsApp and Facebook are the source of news and information, parties take their digital presence seriously. Almost every major political party has several WhatsApp groups, Facebook pages and Twitter accounts from which they post content actively and share live information. Major parties like the BJP and AAP have social media teams to produce and share content. A few politicians like Jayant Sinha and Meenakshi Lekhi have gone as far as to launch their own constituency-level mobile phone applications to better communicate their message of development and progress to their constituents.

Historically, political leaders and parties have spent extravagant sums to spread their message. Parties spend crores of rupees on posters, radio messages and hoardings, to make sure the voter knows what they stand for. One can see the commitment parties bring to communicating their message by analysing election expenditure (see graph below). You will notice that with time, parties have been willing to spend more and more on ensuring that voters are getting the desired message.

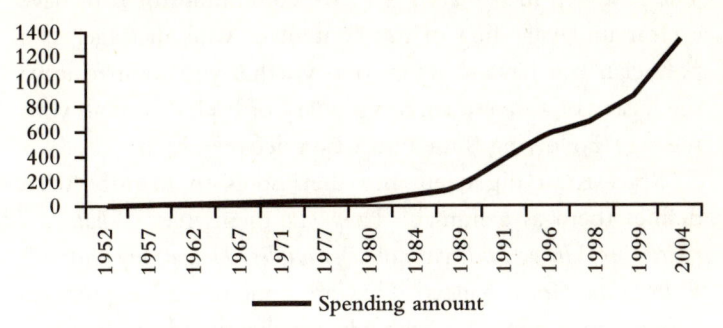

```
1400
1200
1000
 800
 600
 400
 200
   0
      1952 1957 1962 1967 1971 1977 1980 1984 1989 1991 1996 1998 1999 2004
                          ▬▬ Spending amount
```

Until 1989, overall election spending remained under 200 crore rupees. There was a huge jump in election expenditure post-1989, following which we see a sharp upward curve after 2004[4]. The general elections of 2014, as per reporting by the *Wall Street Journal*, saw an expenditure of thirty thousand crore rupees or more on elections. A significant part of election expenditure is to poll people's opinions and to understand their sentiment, in order to craft a message that resonates with them. This involves printing posters that are put up across districts and cities, renting hoarding space to drape party slogans, and the publication of newspaper advertisements. Strong communication is critical in politics.

As an aspiring politician, it is important that you recognize this and work actively to hone your communication skills. This section focuses on explaining the art of communication, providing tips on how to strengthen your communication capacities. Specifically, it will focus on three distinct features: crafting your message, delivering a good speech and finding the right channels to do so.

[4] Election Commission of India: http://eci.nic.in/eci_main1/expenditurel_loksabha.aspx

Art of Communication

The first step in being an effective communicator is to have a clear understanding of the content of your message. As a politician you have to figure out whether you want to leave the legacy of a statesman, or visionary or leader through your message. Following is the distinction between each:

Statesmen dig deep into their souls to identify what defines them as a human. They ask themselves: *What do I believe in? Why do I believe in those principles? How do my principles fit in to the current context?* They are remembered as pioneers because they come up with ideas, policies and programmes that take humanity in a progressive direction. A statesman would be someone like Gandhi who had faced discrimination and violence in his formative years. These experiences helped him identify his values and eventually he became an advocate of the non-violence movement, the flagship protest against the British.

Visionaries look outward and craft their messages after getting a sense of the people's needs. They are driven by the need to help people and to make society better. Leaders like Abraham Lincoln would be considered visionaries, because of his ability to mobilize people against slavery in the United States. His tenure as president involved drafting legislation that pushed for the abolishment of slavery. He had a vision for an equitable world.

Leaders can follow the trodden path well. They build their messages by sticking to the party line, following others in their wake. They pass on messages they have heard from seniors in the party in different public fora. Though unexceptional in their thought, they are effective in executing the path laid out for them. This wins them the allegiance of others in the party, and they are able to rise within the party though they are not memorable. Some leaders might customize the message to suit current contexts but for the most part, party leaders are likely to repeat the party line.

As you figure out how you would want to craft your message, let's take a deeper look on ways to frame messages.

1. Looking internally: Each person has a powerful narrative. Our experiences of pain and suffering or conquest form the basis of our core principles. You have to be mindful of these. Take note of your experiences to use in the future for messaging. Identify the moments that shape your principles and use them to inspire others.

   Narendra Modi, in the lead up to the general elections of 2014, was able to develop a brilliant core message drawing from his life experiences. His message, his core principles and the reason he believed in them – he was able to communicate this in a simple and clean manner.

   He articulated that he comes from humble roots and thus represents the average Indian and understand the voters' pain. He has an established track record as three-term chief minister of Gujarat and can deliver development to overcome that pain. Every voter knew this about the man who is now prime minister. He was successful not only in communicating stories from his past, but also in working it into a larger message through all his major campaign speeches. These stories ranged from simple references to his travels across India as a young man to his experiences during his time as chief minister of Gujarat.

   If one were to compare Rahul Gandhi to Narendra Modi, one would notice that Gandhi fails to share any of his own experiences. He does not speak about losing his father, uncle and grandmother, or the perils of needing to prove himself in politics. This leaves the voter disconnected to his messaging.

Rahul Gandhi could change his messaging to sound like this – I come from a background of public servants. My grandmother died to protect India, my father was killed by terrorists and my mother has pledged her life to ensure that our political tapestry remains intact. From each of these people, I have learned. But most importantly, as a youth leader, I have learned from you, travelling across villages and cities to understand the aspirations of people.

Being open about one's narrative and turning each life experience into a strength allows one to develop a strong political message.

2. Looking externally: 'The key to winning an election is understanding the pulse of the people,' an experienced campaign manager explained to me. 'If you are able to recognize the needs of the voter, you are likely to win the election, but if you can understand their dreams, you will win by a landslide,' he concluded. Political parties spend a terrific amount of money to gauge public sentiment through polling. But this science of polling is still developing in India, and individuals with insight on voter sentiment are still tremendously valuable.

This is where the brilliance of leaders like Indira Gandhi can be seen. In the 1970s, the INC was struggling. Indira knew that she would not win the election without tapping into the hearts and minds of people. With a strong team and keen political acumen, Indira introduced two policies that changed voter perception. At each rally and meeting, Indira would discuss the removal of privy purses and the nationalization of Indian banks.

Indira knew that the election could be sealed only with the votes of the poor. By abolishing the privy purse enjoyed by some rulers and by nationalising banks, she demonstrated that she was willing to serve the poorest of the poor. 'She would intentionally wander into a crowd and touch people because she wanted to make the poor feel that she was one of them,' a senior journalist who followed Indira through the campaign explained.

The ability to understand the voter and serve them through policies can be transformative if the discourse is taken beyond elections. Nitish Kumar recognized the importance of capturing the women's vote and realized that alcohol abuse was a major problem in Bihar. Accordingly, he promised an alcohol-free household during the elections in 2015. The message resonated with women and he was re-elected chief minister that year. He continued to deliver on his promise, winning the allegiance of women voters. It is important to have a strong gauge of community needs.

3. Follow the party line: Most politicians follow the party line when framing their campaign messages. Think tanks and senior leaders within the party provide an overview of the party's stances and leaders repeat the same when speaking to the public. If a leader can articulate these messages strongly, then s/he can rise within the party.

The current party spokesperson of the Congress, Sanjay Jha, was able to establish his credibility by defending the Congress in a difficult time and toe the party line. Jha was the founder of CricInfo, a prominent website that offered insights and analysis on cricket and other sports. He was well-known in media circles and was often invited to panel discussions on cricket and sports. After enrolling in the Congress as a party worker, he did not sit still. Instead, he started a website called Humara Congress that collated opinions and pieces about the Congress and its performance. He wrote opinion pieces on social, economic and political issues on the platform as well, consistent with the party line.

In 2012, when Congress was ridden by scandals and faced a hard time in public opinion, several Congress party workers and leaders refused to come on television to defend the party. But Jha was willing to do so. He was called into discussions, having been on television panels before. Over the course of several months, he fearlessly battled opponents of the Congress on prime time news channels. It was challenging, but he did it.

The Congress party rewarded Jha for speaking the party line and he was promoted to be the party spokesperson. As you can see, speaking the party line can be rewarding, but limits the sort of leader you will be. To be a visionary or a statesman you will have to look beyond.

Most political leaders frame their message by combining the methods listed above. They all begin by asking themselves what they wish to achieve through messaging. Figure out what you want to say so that you can work on *how* to say it.

Constructing a Good Speech

In Indian politics, speeches represent not just an opportunity to convey your ideas but are symbolic of your standing

HOW TO BUILD YOUR BRAND AND MESSAGE?

within the party. Senior leaders are expected to sit on events and speak. Your ability to speak is a critical component of your political career. Unfortunately, there is no standardized structure to a speech, but as an aspiring politician, you have to dissect speeches you hear and learn key components from them to use in your own speeches.

This section will share two examples of exceptional speeches and illustrate how to dissect and study them. We will look at Modi's speech from Madison Square Garden and Barack Obama's speech at the 2004 National Democratic Convention. Let us begin by looking at PM Modi's speech (which is available on YouTube).

Modi's speech in Madison Square Garden wove in humour, honesty and humility. He used narratives and shared numbers. He thumped the table, waved his arms, changed his intonation and (best of all) spoke impromptu for over two hours. At the end he received a standing ovation, and more importantly, won the hearts of his listeners. How did he do it?

How does Prime Minister Modi speak with such passion, without fumbling for notes or a teleprompter? How does he use humour in unexpected ways, without forgetting his next point? How does he transition smoothly from one point to the next and with such ease? After listening to several of his speeches and analysing the structure of his content, I have put together a brief list of six of the most brilliant techniques he consistently adopts. They are as follows:

1. **The Art of Starting Strong**: The prime minister is proud of India's civilizational history, our demographic advantages, and the progress we have made from being a country of black magic to becoming a cradle of technology. He begins every speech by affirming his

faith in India and the promise it holds. While this might seem like an obvious way to begin a speech for any prime minister, the zeal with which he conveys his patriotism is a terrific technique. His emphatic praise of India and Indians instils an immediate sense of pride in those listening to him. We begin to believe that Indians are great, and that there is so much we should be proud off. He exudes optimism that is immediately engaging.

2. **Alliterations and Sound-Bites, or the Art of Phrasing**: 'Make in India', 'Democracy, Demography and Demand' and 'Swachh Bharat' are few of the many phrases that Modi has mentioned in his term as prime minister. The audience is able to relate to him when he communicates difficult goals in sound-bites. The use of such phrases can be a particularly powerful technique when addressing large audiences, as it simplifies complex goals while also making them catchy. People can remember two words and this makes it easier for people to take away key ideas. The toughest part of using these sound-bites is to come up with them!

3. **Empower People, or the Art of Engaging**: Raise your son right, keep India clean, nominate ideas, says the prime minister's website, as part of engaging his listeners to engage with him. Sociologists suggest that the most effective way of engaging people in any campaign is to give them avenues to be active agents (as opposed to passive observers). Modi thrives on announcing specific ways in which citizens can engage. For example, when he tells me that I am expected to talk about India's successful mission to Mars for just 5 minutes at my place of work, I feel as though I am contributing to India's success!

4. **Tangible Deliverables, or the Art of Promising**: To ask people to open bank accounts, build toilets, and sweep railway stations are deceitfully simple requests. Yet it is their simplicity that helps garner overwhelming support. The ability to focus on 'real solutions' (and *not* problems) is an undervalued virtue in politics. The assumption is that heads of states are expected to provide 'high level ideas.' But Modi has been ground breaking in focusing on tangible deliverables. The ability to provide tangible solutions in a speech can be amazing!
5. **Speak with Your Body, or the Art of Communicating**: Prime Minister Modi's eyes glow when he speaks about the promise that the country holds, he thumps his hands when excited and he looks from side to side to address the whole audience. The ability to communicate not just through your words but also your actions resonates with listeners. We don't just listen to him now, but also see the excitement he emanates.
6. **End on a High Note or the Art of Leaving an Audience Fascinated**: Consistently, the prime minister saves major announcements for the very end of his speech. In Madison Square Garden, he waited till the very end to announce changes in visa policies. His speech is structured to hold the best for last, leaving listeners with a feel-good factor as he exits, making him even more likeable. This also keeps the audience engaged until the end.

The six points above are a few of many factors that make the Modi's speeches as prime minister memorable. Other factors include his use of humour, his subtle bragging about his humble background, and his optimistic tone. If you want to strengthen your public speaking skills, I strongly recommend that you study Narendra Modi's speeches and their structure.

Barack Obama's speeches are also of great value. One of Obama's finest speeches was delivered at the Democratic National Convention of 2004 (and is available on YouTube for your reference). He maintained a simple three-piece structure throughout this speech, but the content of his speech was phenomenal. The structure is as follows:

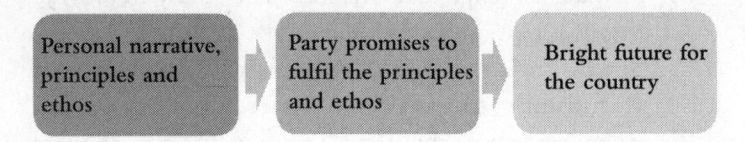

Personal narrative, principles and ethos → Party promises to fulfil the principles and ethos → Bright future for the country

1. Personal Narrative: The story of an underdog resonates with all of us. We are hopeful when we hear about the unlikeliest of candidates succeeding. Obama starts his speech as the story of the underdog. His grandparents worked through the Great Depression to survive. His father was a migrant from Kenya and his mother a middle-class woman. Their family was middle-class and he worked hard through his life. Even though he is a black man, he was able to rise up because he lived in America. The US represents the land of meritocracy and hard work, values that he grew up believing in. Narrating his story simply, Obama highlights these values and blows the audience away. He makes his story relatable. The ability to look deep and develop a narrative that will resonate with the audience is an incredibly powerful tool.
2. Party Promises: Even though the personal narrative can be powerful, it is important not to spend too much time on it. Following this mantra, Obama shifts from his

personal narrative to the promises of the Democratic Party. He speaks of its achievements in making the US meritocratic by giving opportunities to everybody. He weaves his speech with his experience of meeting with average Americans and listening to their joys and concerns. He talks of the factory worker and the minimum wage worker, and what he heard from them when he met them. He pulls together his experiences by stating that the Democratic Party exists to fulfil the promises of these people. The mention of the party turns the focus from his personal ethos to the progress of the country.

3. Bright Future: Obama completes his speech with a hopeful message of a bright future. He talks about the US being a promising country with infinite potential. He also speaks of how the right leadership can boost the country forward. The ability to leave on a high note makes the audience walk away with a positive feeling.

Obama and Modi are only two of other phenomenal speakers. As you plan on entering politics, it is important that you construct your own speeches mindfully. Remember that you must:

- Have a key message that you hope to communicate (positive messages tend to be more powerful).
- Personalize what you are sharing with your audience and tell them why what you are saying is important to you.
- Speak with your body and not just your words (move your hands, and express emotions with your face)
- Ask your audience to do something for the country (for example, to be proud, or to stand united).

It is only with all of the above in mind that you can move forward as a good speaker. Speaking is critical to your political career and you must master it.

Let us turn to a brief discussion on where to communicate.

Where to communicate?

In today's world, not only what you communicate but the medium of your communication matters. Social media, television, grassroots campaigns, parliamentary debates, rallies and focus group conversations are a few media available to communicate with your audience. Each context has its own benefits and has to be thought through in terms of a larger communication strategy. Find below a few questions you will want to consider in thinking through the mode of communication you will choose:

- Who do you want to communicate with? Will this medium reach them?
- Do you want this to be a direct message to your target demographic? Will it make sense to involve a third-party to come in and ask tough questions to make the message more objective?
- What do you want the audience to take away?

Are you a good communicator?

As you think of your way forward in the political sphere, it is important that you take a step back to understand your core message and how you want to communicate it. Evaluate your current skills with those you will need to build. Here is a table with some sample skills. Run down the list and check how many skills you have and identify the gaps:

Description of Skill	Expand your answers to 3-4 sentences
Do I understand what my core principles and beliefs are that will feed my communication?	
What are the avenues I want to engage to communicate?	
Who am I going to target through my political communication?	
What will be the key take-away of my communication?	

A speechwriter from the Obama Administration once spoke of how Obama spent several hours crafting each of his speeches. Obama would sit in his office late into the night and rewrite drafts. This shows us that even the most articulate people in the world put in time and effort to ensure that they communicate well. Speaking and writing is about practice, and as an aspiring politician you must devote time and energy to this practice.

Chapter 6

How Do You Make Money When in Politics?

Political parties and the government in India do not provide a salary or any compensation to politicians and elected officials. An aspiring politician devotes a majority of their time to politics to ensure a successful career, and makes efforts to work closely with the party and community members to gain political capital. This limits the time and energy they can then devote to earning a comfortable living.

It is unfortunate that at present there is no system that compensates party workers committed to political work for their time. Political parties rarely provide compensation. This does not bode well for young professionals aspiring to enter politics. Financial constraints continue to be a major deterrence. Politics is even harder for aspirants when they are expected to support party members and constituents. It is especially hard on those who hope to contest elections, as they have to raise money for their campaigns.

With these pressures in place and no financial support network for aspiring politicians, it is unsurprising that even the most talented professionals choose not to enter the field. Political parties justify the lack of financial support by saying that party members are supposed to be volunteers who cannot expect financial compensation. The unfortunate result of the lack of financial support often means that several politicians make money illegally. And so, unethical political practices arise and persist.

Even though our systems make it difficult to be righteous about making a transparent earning while in politics, there has been a legacy of ethical statesmen, visionaries and leaders who have found ways of making money the legal way. As an aspiring politician who plans to live ethically, you should think carefully about your source of income early in your career. Most sincere politicians maintain a separate source of income through professional services such as consultancy in law, medicine and so on. They plan, prepare and then proceed. As you think about politics ask yourself whether you:

- Understand the cost related to entering politics.
- Have a plan in place to make money and savings through appropriate means.
- Have prepared financially for the possible costs you might incur.

Reading this chapter will not be enough. Your 'To do' should include:

- Honing skills and networks that will allow for you to freelance (when necessary).
- Saving for your political future.
- Living a humble lifestyle to be more efficient with resources.

Looking back...

On 8 March 1889, Biswanath Das was born in Ganjam, Odisha. He came from a landowning family and inherited significant wealth. He could have lived a comfortable life, but Das had a higher calling. He wanted to give back to his community through public service. Born in the backdrop of the independence movement, he was keen on contributing to the story. And so he did.

Das pursued his higher education at Ravenshaw College and Calcutta University and went on to study law. During his student life, he enrolled in the INC and even stood for elections for legislative council. Das was eventually elected to the Madras Legislative Council for three terms, but resigned during his third term as his disgruntlement with the British government grew. His tenure as a leader in the independence movement began after his resignation.

Even though Das belonged to the landowning community, he could see the pain of small farmers. Das plunged into activism and social movements, organizing farmers to demand their rights. He agitated for the oppressed and sought to give them a voice. Soon, Das was recognized as a local leader and representative of the farmers of Odisha. Throughout the independence movement, Das displayed his commitment to the downtrodden and the poorest of the poor, and as India came closer to Independence he was appointed the first chief minister of Odisha.

As India was readying itself to become a republic, an assembly of 299 elected leaders got together to discuss, debate and draw up the Constitution of India. This, the Constituent Assembly, was a platform for some of the greatest Indian thinkers and leaders. They discussed how elections would be held, the separation of powers within the government, and the rights of vulnerable communities. They met for a total of a hundred and seventy-six days over three years. Das, who had gained a strong reputation by the end of the independence movement, was one of the members of the Constituent

Assembly and the only chief minister present on the platform. Each member of the Constituent Assembly had something distinct to say. Das was particularly vocal around the issue of politics and finance.

Even before India was independent, politicians had a complex relationship with money. Most freedom fighters loathed the thought that Viceroys were paid large salaries while the average Indian suffered. When the Constituent Assembly discussed salaries for parliamentarians, several members proposed a minimal stipends for members. Each member of the Constituent Assembly was paid forty-five rupees for each day of attendance. Das was fierce in his opinion on high salaries, and spoke thus in the ornately decorated central hall of parliament:

> 'I am one of those Members who chose to draw only Rs 30. I still feel that Rs 45 a day is too much for a member. I, for myself, a worker, do not need Rs 45 per day. I know there are members in my province who draw their salaries as members of the Assembly and straightaway hand it over to the Secretary of their District Congress committee and receive a scale as fixed by the Congress Committee in preference to the pay that they draw and they go on as whole-time workers.[5]

He was passionate in his commentary against high salaries for parliamentarians.

He echoed Mahatma Gandhi's statements. Gandhi believed that public service should have nothing to do with money. He believed that it necessary to be rooted in humility and devotion to community. Gandhi and Das believed that the salary drawn from the parliamentary and legislative arms of government

---

[5] http://www.frontline.in/static/html/fl2210/stories/20050520002810100.htm

should be given to the party that could and should redistribute the money to party workers. They did, however, discount a few factors.

Das was from a wealthy family background, and had his basic needs met. He led a conservative lifestyle and expected other leaders to do the same. Indian history has often seen leaders like Das with roots in wealthy families, inheriting money and secure of their futures. This has allowed political leaders to sustain their political careers in parliament and ministries. But not everybody in India agrees with the concept that Das argued for about salaries. In India where we hope to have every strata of society represented in parliament, there should be the ability to recruit talent in an open and fair manner. The shackles of financial constraint often limit us. Strong objections were raised in the Constituent Assembly to Das's point. Some members strongly believed that politicians should be fairly compensated.

These members of the constituent assembly were practical. They recognized that money was critical for survival. Frequent discussions took place on money and public service in pre-independence India. In fact, there are several reports of local officials taking bribes to complete tasks. Public officials at the time were poorly paid, and the bribe augmented their income. Even Motilal Nehru expressed grievances about the corruption in British-ruled India. Money and public service have always had a perilous relationship.

In the Constituent Assembly, the views of Gandhi and Das triumphed. A minimal salary was allocated to all elected officials. Over time, there has been an increase in the salary of parliamentarians. But there are some who believe that public service should offer a competitive or high paying salary.

The narrative around public service in India focuses on

living a very humble lifestyle, serving others selflessly, but without considering financial factors. In almost every state, MPs shy away from showing any wealth. The optics of being a poor politician is assumed to be most preferred by voters. This has contributed to the limitations of drawing in a larger pool of leadership talent into politics. Most middle-class Indians are nervous regarding making ends meet and supporting their families if they join politics. They see that politics does not offer enough compensation for the work involved, unless one chooses to be unethical. Several talented leaders steer clear of entering politics for this reason, and politics is then pursued by the wealthy or those unafraid to pursue illegal methods to make money.

Our inability to define the role of money in politics explicitly has been politics' Achilles' heel. It is one of the reasons for rampant corruption amongst elected officials. Consider how much parliamentarians earn as opposed to how much it takes to run for parliamentary office.

The general elections of 2014 is known to be the most expensive one conducted in Indian history. The Centre for Media Studies reported that the election expenditure by political parties was more than 1,400 crores[6] in total. The amount makes Indian elections the second most expensive in the world (the first being the presidential election of 2012 in the US). As elections become expensive, the barriers on entry to politics increase. You need more and more money to run for office, and this leaves behind some of the most talented people. For example, look at how salaries have increased over time, relative to election spending.

[6] http://www.ibtimes.com/indias-2014-election-cost-5-billion-second-only-price-tag-2012-us-presidential-election-1570668

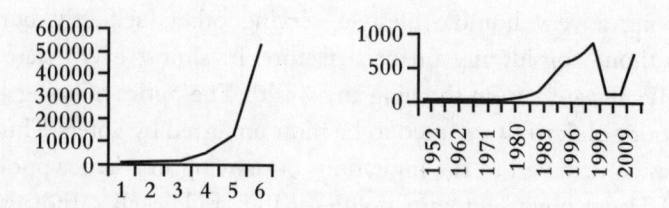

TABLE 6.1: Comparing election spending versus MP salary

Today a parliamentarian takes home fifty-two thousand rupees per month in salary. The ADR estimates that the average parliamentarian has to spend one crore to win an election. Even if s/he saves her/his entire salary over five years, they will have only raised 30 per cent of what they need. Actual spending during elections are hard to research since the amounts spent are often undisclosed. The financial expectations from our elected representatives are severely flawed.

For aspiring politicians who are not in office, finances are even more complicated. With the exception of the BJP and CPI(M), parties do not pay volunteers or members. However, if you plan on having a realistic chance to get an election ticket, you will be expected to devote most of your time to politics. If you are trying to climb the political ladder, there is no financial support available. In this context, you have to be creative about how you raise resources and plan your financial future.

The exceptional parties...

A party volunteer is expected to work toward fulfilling the party ideology driven by passion. Party positions are therefore, voluntary. Even if you rise within the ranks in the party system, it is unlikely that you will be paid. Most parties do not offer any financial support to their members. Consequently, they do not attract the best talent. The BJP and CPI(M) are exceptions to such practices. They have a relatively strong cadre-based culture as well as systems of meritocracy. Both these parties recognize finances as a key part of a person's functioning, and have introduced a financial compensation system for select members in their cadre. Find below details on each party's innovation: :

- BJP and members of RSS: The BJP is a relatively meritocratic party. BJP leadership gauges the commitment of party members to the ideology and organization in giving out election tickets. The BJP also works with the RSS to recruit promising talent. The RSS provides support to some of its committed members who reach the senior ranks of pracharak, providing a basic stipend of a few thousand rupees and a place to stay. Leaders recognize that most people do not have a source of earning and provide a basic stipend. Several leaders including the Prime Minister Narendra Modi have spent a significant portion of their careers working at the grassroots, canvassing and creating a support base for the BJP as pracharaks.
- CPI(M) cadre: The CPI(M) believes in empowering the people. Members are expected to commit fully to furthering the communist cause. Following the model mentioned by Mahatma Gandhi, the CPI(M) supports its committed members by expecting 'earning' members such as parliamentarians, to redistribute their salary within the party and party workers. Parliamentarians from the CPI(M) do so and take

home a meagre sum. In a conversation with Ritabrata Banerjee, a CPI(M) member in the Rajya Sabha, I had asked, 'How do you manage by giving away one lakh rupees to your party and sustaining on only twenty-five thousand rupees? Doesn't it bother you to have have so little remaining for yourself?' He smiled at me and answered, 'Why does one need more money than that to run a household?' CPI(M) prescribes a very humble lifestyle to its members and this is evident in their earning expectations.

You can see that only two major parties provide any financial support to political workers and aspirants. The scale of this support is minimal, only a few thousand rupees. The political system needs to reflect on this gap and come up with an effective solution promptly if it aims to bring in new talent.

In this context, how do we expect ethical and corruption-free politicians to emerge from a system that does not talk explicitly about money as an issue for aspiring politicians? How would politicians cover their existing costs if they work full time as party members without any pay? Beyond elections, what are the other hidden costs for aspiring politicians?

In India, most of our conversations often revolve around corruption when we think of money and politics. But we rarely try to understand why this is the case. Our current political landscape provides limited support from the party for political aspirants. In countries like Singapore or the US, institutions have been built to support young emerging leaders.

In the US, you can join politics as an aide to a Senator or as a representative to learn about the political system, build social capital, and eventually run for office without compromising yourself financially. Eventually when you decide to run for political office, the Democratic and Republican National Parties have strong connections with funders and donors, and leaders within each of these parties help make the appropriate introductions for a candidate to fundraise for an election campaign. In fact, one of Barack Obama's greatest strengths was his ability to reach out to donors and raise funds for his campaign when running for president. The Clinton family is also known to have deep connections with corporate donors. Through dinners, lunches and one-on-one meetings, each presidential candidate invites prospective donors and speaks to them on why they should contribute money to their campaigns. Those who are convinced support the candidates.

In India, corporate funding of elections has been banned. The issue of money is so sensitive that when I was conducting research for this chapter, no politician or expert went on record in speaking of the role money played in their careers. Most denied that money was an issue or pretended they had enough support and did not need to worry about finances. That made the chapter hard to work on. Nonetheless, it was the nebulous nature surrounding issues of finance that pushed me harder to bring the topic out into public discussion.

As you enter politics, begin by understanding where you will require financial resources. It is important that you prepare yourself financially and understand the investments required for politics. In the next section, you will learn about the costs involved in politics.

Where Do You Need Money in Politics?

'When you join politics, people assume that you are rich and have money to give away,' a senior political leader once told me. 'I find party workers in my office everyday asking for money. I am barely able to satisfy them when my constituents walk into my office with a litany of their demands. From a daughter's marriage to a father's medical treatment to a brother's scholarship, I end up giving out at least one lakh rupees a month to people in need. I have to do this because I am a politician. If I don't support people when they are most in need, they will not vote me into office when I stand for election the next time. You have to show the voter that you have the intent to help them in their time of need. And voters think that I am a rich man,' the leader confessed. He owned a small business in the district and had been relying on his family wealth to support his political ambitions. The leader told me that people began asking him for money well before he was elected and made it into parliament, when he had just begun conversations with party leaderships of the possibilities of getting an election ticket.

It is evident from the politician's commentary that leaders have to dip in to their savings or sources of wealth to support their ambitions.

The political leaders I have interviewed have had to work within the party system anywhere between six months as with the case of Mani Shankar Aiyar, to eight years as with the case of Jairam Ramesh, before they made it into parliament. During this period, they have had to find creative ways of earning money. Once they have been offered a ticket, they have had to worry about raising money for elections. Once they have won the elections, they have had to worry about supporting their family, constituency and party on meagre salaries.

As a first step, it is important for you to map out where you will require financial resources in your political career. The figure below marks out every stage of your political career that you will have to worry about in terms of financial resources.

Financial worries in different stages:

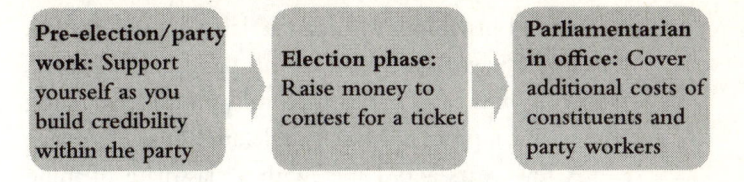

Pre-election/party work: Support yourself as you build credibility within the party	➤	Election phase: Raise money to contest for a ticket	➤	Parliamentarian in office: Cover additional costs of constituents and party workers

- *Pre-Election Phase:* 'Our founding fathers didn't envision politics being a full-time profession. In fact, most people who drafted the Indian Constitution viewed politics as a noble calling that a select few people would join for a few years only to return to their fulltime professions,' said Vikram Lal, a political commentator. The nature of politics has changed over time.

  Politics is a full-time commitment and like any other profession, requires ongoing engagement, learning and growth. Some of our most efficient politicians have had full-time experience in politics for several years before becoming heads of states. This includes our current prime minister Narendra Modi, EMS Namboodripaad (the first chief minister of Kerala) and Chandra Babu Naidu, the chief minister of Andhra Pradesh. In the case of Modi, he started his career in the RSS.

  One of the assignments given to Modi as an RSS worker was to travel across India and understand the status of BJP cadre. On his travels, he met with thousands of people and in the process gained management skills to diagnose problems and come up with possible solutions. The experience was fundamental to helping him understand how party structures work. L.K. Advani brought Modi in to organize a pad yatra and this tested his ability to organize large groups people. As an RSS worker, Modi had his basic costs covered, allowing him to invest himself fully in understanding the political process. Most people are not as fortunate.

A few years ago, I met with a classmate of mine who had been an active politician for five years. He had graduated from a top engineering college and had worked with a multi-national company before deciding to enter politics. He joined a regional party but had been operating out of Delhi. 'Money is better in Delhi,' he explained.

'How so?' I asked.

'After my first year of joining the party I was excited. The party leaders told me that they saw potential in me and asked me to continue working in my district. They said that if I could build the local cadre, I would be given a ticket in the upcoming elections. I wanted to do right by the party and not exploit relationships to curry favours and make money. Instead I lived off my savings for the first two years. I was running out of money and hoped that they would give me a ticket in the state elections. They said they had bigger plans and asked me to be patient. I thought they were referring to parliamentary elections. I stayed patient. I reached out to my parents for support because I didn't have any savings left. They hesitated but obliged.

'I continued to work hard. Parliamentary elections came and went but I didn't get a ticket. I was upset. But I didn't want to lose hope. I had no money and no prospects. But right after the election, a small businessman approached me. His project was stuck with the state government. He said he would give me a handsome sum if I could get it through. I knew the minister of that department well. He was a dear friend and we had worked together on a few campaigns.

'I scheduled a meeting with him and within days, the projects went through. I made more than I could have imagined. Now that I am in Delhi, I have a lot more businessmen like that approaching me. I can support my family while I continue to hope for the ticket. There has been a change in party leadership and they are saying that I am likely to get a ticket in the next election,' he told me, hopefully. His story about the quiet but dangerous entry of vested interest in politics is not new. It marks one of the most frequent ways in which politicians fall prey to corruption.

Businesses approach political leaders to push for projects to come through with the offer of bribes. Aspiring politicians become a key part of this lobbying process. The example of my old classmate is only one of many examples of the relationship between business and politics.

As an ethical politician, you will have to prepare to not fall victim to such a system. For professionals like lawyers and doctors, there is the distinct possibility of continuing their practice while pursuing politics. For example, Kakoli Ghosh Dastidar is a trained doctor and Lok Sabha MP from West Bengal. She continues to run a clinic in addition to her work in parliament. This is hard for a salaried professional.

If you work for a multi-national firm or a service company, you are expected to maintain work hours.

This does not bode well for your political career that requires flexible hours. As a first step, remember that you will have to freelance through several years of your work to earn an income, and assess the resources you have in hand. If you have an independent practice or business, build the capacity of the business to run without your presence. If you are a salaried professional, consider consulting positions.

- *Election-phase:* Elections are an expensive affair. The Election Commission (EC) has a spending limit of forty lakh rupees for parliamentary elections. However, candidates have to spend at least one crore rupees for Lok Sabha elections based on deductions from informal conversations around the general elections of 2014. Posters, television advertisements, and public events require a month or two of tremendous investment from any candidate for any certainty of victory. This also means that your investment might not yield any return.

  Select candidates go a step further and invest in services like polling and political campaign management, further increasing election budgets. In southern states like Andhra and Tamil Nadu, the budget for parliamentary elections are as high as twenty crore rupees (and this data point is arrived at on the basis of hearsay). The defiance of the spending limits mandated by the EC are common in political circles. In fact, Atal Bihari Vajpayee once said that most political careers often begin with a lie, as candidates always misreport spending to the EC.

  In the general elections of 2014, I had the opportunity to watch the spending patterns in select constituencies quite closely. It was fascinating to see how quickly and promptly expenditures added up. On any given day, the candidate would start out by pointing that 'little things' like posters and newspaper ads were missing. A few lakhs rupees were spent on acquiring those. This would promptly be followed by the need to have more cars, people, office space and additional logistical support on the ground. A few more lakhs were spent in the afternoon. By the evening, decisions would be made that there was a need for more rallies and public events. The local party workers would get together and plan out a series of events over evening tea. By the end of tea-time, they would ask for more money from the candidate. The candidate would hand out several lakh rupees. Sprinkled through the day were additional party workers asking the candidate for money for various other support pieces.

By the end of the campaign, it was unsurprising that the candidate had spent a few crore rupees. Most candidates get some amount of financial support from the party. But this is often much less than what they require (maybe 10 per cent of their entire costs). They then look to their own savings. Finally, they seek support from local businesses and other vested interests for campaigns. 'The last month of a campaign is when parties are willing to spend through their noses to ensure political victory,' a businessman running a public relations firm shared with me.

Unfortunately, we have very little information on how money in Indian elections are raised: who the potential donors are and how they are sought. The results are stories like that of Mayawati who claimed her 'supporters' funded her campaign. The only party actively working toward campaign finance reform in recent political history has been the AAP. The AAP initially listed online the names of all those who had supported them, created an online portal to solicit donations and held lunches and dinners with high net-worth individuals to seek financial support. This culture has already dwindled.

ADR is a non-profit based out of Delhi that has been pushing for increased financial transparency in political parties. ADR has gone so far as to file lawsuits against political parties, demanding that they be considered public entities and therefore are required to disclose financial assets. Unfortunately, the court favoured political parties. There continues to be a push for financial transparency around political parties.

Hope emerged after the demonetization policy was announced in November 2016, and the Modi Administration pushed for all transactions to be made through legitimized bank accounts. Cash donations to political parties obfuscate tracking. The sudden push toward white money made it harder for political parties to garner funds. ADR has reported that nearly three quarters of income for national parties come from unknown sources: cash is king in political circles.

After demonetization, stories emerged of how political leaders with rooms full of thousand rupee notes were in a conundrum, trying to turn black money into white. In light of this, the Chief Election Commissioner Nasim Zaidi pushed for reform in political finance. With the pressure from civil society organizations, Finance Minister Arun Jaitley announced that donations above two thousand rupees would need to be accepted through cheque or wire transfers. Critics are not convinced that this will bring tangible change.

As you enter politics, you will have to think carefully on how you want to run your campaign. Will you expect the community to fund the campaign? Have you saved enough wealth for yourself? How will you maximize your resource allocation? AAP has proven that the amount of money spent on election does not decide electoral victory. It is as much about resource allocation, i.e., recognising where to channel resources the most. There are some critical questions to ask yourself as you think about contesting for elections.

- *In-office phase:* 'Last week, I had a distraught father come to my office. His daughter's wedding was in a few days and he needed money. I felt for him and instructed my office to give him fifty thousand rupees,' said R.K. Jena, MP from Balasore. Jena is one of the top-five of wealthy Indian politicians. Despite having a significant amount of wealth, he feels the pinch of financial pressure of being in office. Every parliamentarian I have met has shared stories about how s/he has had to spend money on their constituency either through party workers or constituents.

'Being in office requires a lot of money,' explained a senior Congress party member. 'You have a lot of hidden costs, including raising money for your party and covering costs for your party members. In some instances, you might have the chief minister of your party coming to your state and you are asked to organize a rally. This means you will have to bear the costs,' he concluded.

At the beginning of your career, these costs are not of concern. You do need to be mindful of limited financial resources and how they will shape your years in office. Some parliamentarians are phenomenal at raising funds from corporate partners and foundations to support their constituents, and this might be one of the skills you would want to polish.

As you think about the financial difficulties, it is also important to think about possible options to offset them. The next section describes a few ways to make money ethically while sustaining your political ambitions.

What Are the Ways You Can Make Money?

There have been some established ways in which aspiring politicians maintain financial independence while pursuing politics full-time. Following are some of the ways that successful politicians have previously supported themselves.

Running your own business: It is fairly common to see established businessman like Rahul Bajaj or Rajeev Chandrasekhar enter parliament. Established businessmen have significant capital to fund their own campaigns and the flexibility to run their businesses while attending to parliamentary work. Beyond the large business leaders, there are also some politicians who run small and medium-sized businesses.

Nadim Ul Haque is the owner of an Urdu newspaper. Ul Haque is based out of Kolkata where he devotes more than half his time to running this business. He reports that his business has suffered a bit since parliament requires a lot of his attention. But he earns enough to maintain his lifestyle and support his family. Ul Haque is one of the owners of a medium-sized business from parliament. You can consider starting and/or establishing your own business before joining politics to ensure a steady source of income.

Continuing in your professional work: Doctors, lawyers and similar professionals have the advantage of being able to run independent practices to ensure a source of income. Kapil Sibal and Ram Jethmelani continued their legal practice despite being parliamentarians. Then there are doctors like Dr Sanjay Jaiswal who runs his medical practice, seeing a few patients a week in his community.

Most professionals will tell you that their work takes a hit when they get involved in politics. Sometimes, they will make money enough to support their families

Freelancing and part-time work: There are several part-time opportunities that skilled professionals can do to ensure a decent income, especially in development work and journalism. Both Jairam Ramesh and Mani Shankar Aiyar were writers for weekly newspapers before making it to parliament. Several party spokespersons and members are often columnists for leading publications and are paid decent money.

Several senior Congress leaders worked for the World Bank and United Nations, conducting research, analysis and writing papers. These positions provide a pay cheque but do not require strict office hours. A number of my old classmates who are currently in politics are consultants at the World Bank and are paid on a daily basis.

Opportunities of work to support government: A new trend is emerging in governance where the government is opening up and bringing in lateral talent through paid positions. For example, parties are appointing volunteers to government positions. In Delhi, the office of the chief minister's office has inducted a number of party members as advisors to ministries in government. Advisors have policy backgrounds and are qualified professionals, working directly with ministers to support their everyday responsibilities. Similarly, the state government of has brought on board talented volunteers who have graduated from top Universities in the US to come on board as political advisors. This culture is laudable because it gives people an official designation and fewer financial worries.

Appointing political supporters in advisory roles is common in politics in the US. If adopted correctly, it can empower the administration and ensure a channel of lateral entry. It can incentivize entry into parties for talented Indians. Times to come will tell how such programmes will be adopted and how they will fare.

There are also opportunities in firms like Chanakya and Political Edge that are electoral management companies recruiting young and talented professionals. These firms pay well while giving young people an 'inside look' of politics. They provide opportunities to participate in campaigns and understand various components of elections while ensuring payment. This model is common in the US, where elected officials bring their experience of working in firms such as these, into politics. The firms give them necessary and useful exposure to the life of elected representatives, allowing them to prepare for the future.

There are ways of earning money ethically in politics. However, it is important that you plan, prepare and process.

Reflecting on the Present State

It is important that you think about your financial standing before entering the political sphere. Make a realistic assessment of your financial assets and skills, and the avenues for further earning that you can consider. Ensure that you do not have to drop out of politics because of financial trouble. Run down the list in the table below to check how you fare.

Financial Status	Yes/No	How will I work towards this? Add a timeline
Do I have savings that I can use in case I can't earn money after joining a party?		
Do I have any skills, that I can leverage to support my income base?		
Do I have realistic expectations about how frugally I will have to live after I join a party?		
Do I understand the financial repercussions of joining the political system?		

SECTION III
Preparing Emotionally for Politics

Chapter 7

What Are the Personal Tolls of Politics?

Politics is an all-consuming profession that takes a toll on one's personal life. Most aspiring politicians spend years as party workers with gruelling work hours on the campaign trail, with late night conversations with party leaders and exhaustive travel with party workers. This process is key to building the social and political capital needed for political growth, but it also takes time away from your family and loved ones. The process can be more frustrating because growth within a political party is hard to assess. Very few political party leaders have a clear sense of if they are making an impact with their bosses and the party. Through such a strenuous process you have to rely on your own emotional strengths, with the support of family and friends around you. Politics is a long journey. As you prepare yourself for entry into politics, it is important that you ask yourself:

- What are the specific costs to my personal life after entering politics?
- How do I plan to balance my personal and political life?
- What can I learn from other politicians to stay mentally strong and emotionally healthy?

Reading this chapter will not be enough. Your 'To do' should include:
- An understanding of how you will build your emotional strength, from veteran politicians.
- Building the trust of your family and friends as you begin to prepare your entry.
- Defining for yourself the reason you have decided to join politics.

Looking Back...

On 15 July 1903, Kumaraswamy and Sivakami welcomed a baby boy to their family who they named Kamaraj. Kamaraj was only learning to walk when his father passed away. The family was heartbroken, but his mother and maternal grandmother vowed to support their little prince in every way possible. Kamaraj would go on to demand a lot of support from his family.

Without a large income in the family, Kamaraj had a challenging childhood. At eleven, disenchanted by what school had to offer and pressed for financial support, he dropped out and started working at his uncle's store. At the time, he heard of India's determined plea for independence from the British. Kamaraj was inspired by what he read in books and newspapers on the Indian independence movement and the valiant fight by freedom fighters. He found himself attending political rallies, and closing the store early to attend political meetings. By the age of sixteen, K. Kamaraj had joined the INC.

Kamaraj would go on to organize meetings and sessions as his family watched wearily, worried about his involvement in politics. By the age of eighteen, he received tremendous attention from other party workers and was considered a rising star within the INC. His worried family decided to send him to Trivandrum. But Kamaraj was to make an even bigger name for himself in Trivandrum.

In Trivandrum, Kamaraj heard of the Vaikom community who were banned from using public resources including roads because of their caste status. He organized protests with party workers against this practice. His family began to demand that he return home when they heard of his activities.

Kamaraj was noticed not only by senior leaders of the INC, but also by the British police. He was arrested four times during the independence movement. In one instance, Kamaraj was framed for attempted murder on the Viceroy of West Bengal, accused of supplying weapons for a pre-planned bombing. Kamaraj needed a lawyer as he could be hanged if convicted, and finally his family sold their ancestral home to pay for legal fees.

After Independence, Kamaraj emerged as a top leader in the INC. He had built the relationships and trust required for political growth. He would go on to become a core member of the leadership in the INC, called the Syndicate. The Syndicate was instrumental in making important decisions, including naming the first prime minister of India.

Kamaraj would go on to work with a man with a very different perception of family and politics: Lal Bahadur, born on 2 October 1904. Like Kamaraj, Lal Bahadur lost his father early, and his case to bubonic plague. His mother moved back in with her family where Lal Bahadur was raised. It was a joint family with several children, and Lal Bahadur saw how his mother's troubles were avoided by the support of an extended family.

Inspired by patriotic teachers and surrounded by the passionate calls of the independence movement, Lal Bahadur began to read about freedom fighters like Bal Gangadhar Tilak and Annie Besant. At the age of eleven he heard Mahatma Gandhi speak about the need for an independent India. He was passionate about this cause. Lal Bahadur dropped out of school to join Gandhi's call for the Quit India Movement.

As a stellar student, Lal Bahadur was to graduate as an exceptional student, and earned the name Shastri, the Hindi word for scholar. Known as Lal Bahadur Shastri, committed to serving the nation's cause, he took an oath of living a simple life and dedicated every moment of his time to his country. He mobilized people to fight for Indian independence and made very little money. At the age of twenty-three, he married Lalitha Devi. By then Lal Bahadur Shastri was already deeply involved in the independence movement and had even been imprisoned for staging protests.

Lal Bahadur Shastri was to spend nine years during the independence movement, away from his wife who raised their children by herself. She never questioned her husband's commitment to politics. Lal Bahadur Shastri faced incredibly difficult times when in prison, with his daughter dying and son falling ill[7]. It was emotionally difficult for Lal Bahadur Shastri to part with his children but his family took on the responsibility.

When Lal Bahadur Shastri came out of prison, he had become a household name. People recognized his commitment and dedication to the country. After the death of Jawaharlal Nehru, Shastri became the second prime minister of independent India. Even as prime minister he continued to rely on his family to endorse his decisions, including when he decided to set up a small farm in his home garden at Delhi to demonstrate the importance of agriculture to the people of India.

[7] http://www.freeindia.org/biographies/greatleaders/shastri/page12.htm

K. Kamaraj and Lal Bahadur Shastri are influential personalities in Indian history, pivotal in structuring our political landscape. They were colleagues who worked tirelessly and selflessly for the country. From being imprisoned by the British to giving countless speeches to mobilize people, they had a difficult political journey. In their work for the Congress, they took several decisions that shaped the course of Indian history. In trying moments in their political journey, they were supported by the support and comfort of their families.

A political journey demands financial, emotional and physical attention. It is an intense journey that very few have been able to complete without the support network of family, friends and mentors who are willing to take up chores and come in to help. Politics is an unpredictable field that has tremendous impact but also demands a lot from an individual.

As you enter the political sphere, it is important that you speak to your family and friends and share with them your dreams. Be sure of why you want to enter politics and convince them of your willingness to go forward in the field. Not all family and friends will agree with your vision but make them understand your perspective and ultimately they will support you. Ask for their input if you are not entirely convinced about your own decision. The support of your family and friends will be the backbone of your political career.

In the following sections you will learn to recognize how politics will take a toll on you and why you will really need your family and friends.

When Will Politics Take a Toll on Your Personal Life?

As a politician, you are expected to represent the voice of the people. It is inevitable that people will surround you, either asking for help or trying to help you (on rare occasions). The people flocking you are citizens you think of as future voters and supporters, and will need to be treated with dignity and respect. You will be expected to entertain their sentiments. With this situation in mind, the living rooms of most aspiring politicians are filled with guests who come with problems, seeking help. 'I would spend over ten thousand rupees a month on tea, milk and snacks,' an aspiring politician complained to me once. 'Eventually I had to cut down on how much snacks I offered,' he continued. 'My wife is the smart one in our relationship. She decided that she would serve the tea and biscuits.'

In addition to potential voters, you are likely to spend significant time with party workers working together on most projects. There is no nine to five in work hours, or strict plans of what you will be expected to do. You will have to gauge the requirements of the party at the time and study your skills to make yourself valuable to party leadership. On one occasion, I was scheduled to have dinner with a senior leader of a regional party. I reached his house at 9: 30 p.m., only to find a room full of party workers. With an upcoming rally to organize, the leader was working on arrangements. I barely saw my dinner host that evening since he was in discussion with party workers until 3 a.m. His son and daughter-in-law were kind enough to entertain us.

The funny thing in politics is that most of the party workers you work with are also your competitors, vying to climb up the party ladder just as you are. Your emotional stability and networks of trust are just that much more important in such a context. When advising parliamentarians and party workers, I have encountered countless calls with party members putting each other down in front of senior leadership to be deemed more worthy of the party ticket and responsibility.

'The structure of our party system makes infighting inevitable. You end up doing political work in a very hostile environment where the person you are working with might end up back stabbing you for a better political future,' a senior politician once confided. 'In this light, you need to come home to people you trust and love,' he went on to say.

As we have seen, the pressures that a political life brings are extremely daunting. The best way that you can prepare yourselves for these challenges is to understand them better. Knowing what will come next will prepare you for it mentally. You will find below some issues faced by politicians.

Lack of Privacy or Personal Time: Every politician, in parliament or not, has several stories of receiving calls in the middle of the night by a disgruntled constituent with complaints. From stories of a wife who ran away to a son who has been arrested, and to a medical emergency, all stories relate the pain that people face. Most politicians acknowledge this as part of the job. Politicians need to be accessible to their voter base and empathetic at the very least. But this can become overwhelming. In one instance, I met an MP who had to leave his house to get away from his constituents.

'I come from a poor district. We don't have any major hospital for miles and those that exist have poor facilities. So when people get sick, they have to come to Delhi. When I just got elected I noticed that most of these people don't have a place to stay in Delhi. They sleep on the roads. I offered a few people my home. Before I could realize what was happening, my house was filled with my constituents. People were sleeping on the floor, sofas, tables and everywhere. It became impossible for my wife and I to stay there.

'We would come home and find people set up in our

bedroom. When we asked them what was happening, they would look at us innocently and say "there is no other place." They are our constituents and in need. I didn't want to question them. A few months in, I turned my house in to a guest house and my wife and I have rented a small apartment in central Delhi,' he told me. 'My voters are important to me and my wife, and I knew that turning our government-allotted home in to a guest house for my constituents was the correct decision. It was going to be more work for my wife to maintain both houses, but you have to do the basic work for your constituents,' he finished. His wife who sat next to him smiled gently, and there was no trace of regret in his voice.

Politicians accept the notion of sacrificing their personal space. Politicians who have been in office for only a few terms expect people to be waiting in their sitting areas at any time of the day. They recognize that in India, where public systems are failing, the elected representative and politician represent hope for vulnerable people. This makes their time public property. This also means that constituents end up taking up what time they have for family and friends.

'My son had his tenth exams coming up, but the house had become a zoo with my husband's constituents present here all the time,' the spouse of a politician complained. 'I finally decided to take him to my parent's house so that he could get some studying done,' she said. Many politicians believe that if you have been in the limelight for long enough, your family adjusts to that lifestyle. 'You have to raise your children to be used to so much attention and your partner has to be your biggest supporter. This journey is difficult and you should take in all the support your family can muster,' explains a senior journalist. There are innumerable stories of spouses who have taken a 'break' from public life and decided to lead separate lives while their partners are in politics. Considering the emotional toll that a politician's career takes, it would be more valuable to stand by your spouse.

Work through your privacy issues with your partner, resolving them together rather treating them as an additional responsibility. Several successful politicians have.

Here are some concerns that you will have to field as you enter into the political sphere.

The difficulty of gauging political growth: Almost no politician can concretely answer the question of how the decision to give a party worker a ticket to contest is made. Instead one is subject to a complicated ideological lesson. 'Electability is important. You have to win the election. The relationship with your party members decides that. So does the presence of a strong brand,' you will hear. But winnability or electability are not defined.

Unlike the private sector, politics does not have a clear direction for growth. You will not know if you are coming closer to being considered for candidature in the elections, and most party leaders will ask for your commitment without offering you a clear sense of where you are headed, or even if you are meeting their expectations. Will holding more rallies help? Will spending more money on hoardings and posters for the party help? There is no metric that determines the selection process. You will need tremendous emotional strength to deal with these insecurities politics brings with itself. Politicians need to surround themselves with optimistic and supportive people.

'I started out in youth politics,' said a BJD worker I spoke to in Odisha. 'People told me I was charismatic and that I had the making of a politician. I passionately believed in the ideals of politics and dived into it headfirst. Party leaders welcomed me into the party and told me to keep working at the grassroots and that eventually I would make for a strong candidate.

'I organized rallies, held meetings, spent countless nights on the campaign trail and even wrote speeches for the candidates. The party leaders would congratulate me and take my name in rallies. They would thank me in person and in public. I would feel happy. But then no designation or reward was extended to me. Instead, each time elections would come around, they would make an excuse about how I just missed the ticket and said I will get it the next time.

'I never understood why I didn't get a ticket and no one explained what I needed to do to get one,' the gentlemen continued. He was forty-two and had given up on politics. After twelve years in the fray, he decided to start his own business. 'My family stood by me when I wanted to pursue politics and when I decided to leave the field to start my own business as well,' he said.

'You have to be very secure in what you are doing. Every politician asks themselves at some point "Why am I doing this? I am putting in a lot of effort and I am neither making money nor climbing the ladder. Is this worth it?"' A senior Congress leader once told me this, and he had been in the party for over three decades.

'I was in the private sector before this and the calculation was simple: you work hard and you will make more money. But in politics you could work as hard as you want but you might still not get anything. That can be really demoralizing. I had to work for close to a decade before the party leadership took note of me,' he completed. As you can see, unlike other more defined paths to success, politics can be an emotionally trying experience.

Senior political leaders emphasize that that it is important to have a social network of people who have faith in you. You might feel dejected and directionless but a partner, family member or friend can really support you and remind you why you chose the life you did.

Cynical environment: Politics is the favourite punching bag for citizens and media houses. When anything goes wrong, the first people to be blamed are politicians (even when it does not involve them). I have personally come across this response several times. When I founded Swaniti and shared with a few colleagues that I was going to work on a social enterprise to support parliamentarians, I saw their expressions change. 'Why would you work with politicians? They are the reason our country is suffering. Maybe removing them from power and bringing in authoritarianism would work better,' said a few of my colleagues from the World Bank. Imagine this: if educated economists have such thoughts, what does the general public think? As an aspiring politician you will face worse.

'I am used to walking in to any meeting and being told my profession consists only of corrupt people. People assume that I am in it only to make money and that I have made it so far in politics because I have a relative or family member who has pulled me through. I am used to being viewed cynically and with suspicion. I have to remember that my goal should be to improve expectations through my demeanour and show them that there are those committed to public service,' said Ijyaraj Singh, an MP from Kota in an elevator full of people slinging abuse at politicians.

Being surrounded by people who look down on your profession can be trying. It can make you reconsider whether what you are doing is valuable. This is why you need to involve your family and friends early on. Explain to them why you think what you are doing is valuable. When you are being tough on yourself, make sure you have the support of loved ones.

Although the pressures of politics are enormous, you do not have to go it alone. Work on creating a strong network of personal support.

How Do You Deal with the Pressures of Politics?

When needy constituents, competitive party workers, opaque leadership and a cynical citizenry surround you, it is difficult to maintain your optimism and passion for politics. Successful politicians need to maintain their calm and composure through such times. Find below some ways in which people have dealt with the pressure.

1. **Ask yourself, 'Why am I doing this?' Involve others in the conversation:** Even the most cynical person will tell you that politicians can define the future of a nation and help those most in need. Remember how a ground breaking policy like the National Rural Employment Guarantee Act influences the lives of millions of people. Governance has an undeniable effect on people and political leaders are the medium of change. When you falter and wonder if you made the right choice, think back to the strongest political leader or role model who has influenced you and remember the level of impact they had. Remember that you joined this field to create that level of impact.

    In her autobiography, Mamata Banerjee often talks of the frustrations she faced when rising through the rungs of the political ladder. Despite being elected to parliament, she felt she was part of the Congress party that was endorsing the tyranny of the ruling communist party in West Bengal. She saw them employ violence and intimidation to win elections. She wanted to do more for her state within the Congress but was pushed down. She had the bigger picture in mind.

Mamata Banerjee took to the streets. In a particularly daring move, she stormed in to the Writer's Building one day and demanded justice for a young woman who had been raped by party workers. She was dragged out of the Writer's Building by her hair. She was later beaten with an iron rod. Mamata was unafraid. She continued to fight and held anti-communist rallies and meetings. The ruling party was angry with her and on several occasions employed hit-men to attack her. Her chant to rid West Bengal of the CPI(M) remained constant.

Several records maintain Mamata often turned to her mother when she battled such strong opposition. Her mother was her source of inspiration and strength. Before any major rally or protest, Mamata would make it a point to touch her mother's feet for her blessings. Her mother would remind her of why she was in this fight. Mamata had terrific mental strength because she kept the bigger picture in mind and because she had a strong champion in her mother.

2. **Dig deep and make it personal:** For political history buffs, it is clear that every political leader has an 'Aha!' moment that leads them to pursue the profession. For example, Mahatma Gandhi came to his own when a British official threw him out of a train because he was a brown man travelling in a compartment that was believed to be a white man's right.

B.R. Ambedkar was defined by the discrimination he faced from upper caste people as a Dalit, when he had to drink from a separate tap to theirs.

When you are emotionally fatigued from political battles and experiences, it is important that you are able to personalize why you went in to politics to begin with. Being able to look through the past and deeply understand the cause of your actions will be important on your political journey. It will no longer be about a higher ideal but about a personal experience that has compelled you to go down this road.

For this you need to introspect on the morals and values that drive you and the experiences that have led you to value them. Several people say their early childhood experiences shape their morals. Dig deep inside your early experiences.

3. **Keep your support network close and remember to value them**: Though the electorate strongly favours leaders like Prime Minister Modi and Atal Bihari Vajpayee who demonstrate complete dedication to public service without immediate family who surround them, a politician cannot work without tremendous support. Throughout the political process, you will need partners and champions who will stand by you and understand your challenges and victories. They will make you feel confident when your faith in yourself flags, acting as an emotional safety net.

In the Indian context, you do not hear much about the presence of the family. In the US, however, the role of the family as a support system is very apparent. Take Barack Obama who despite being the leader of one of the most powerful nations in the world used to find time to sit down to dinner with his wife and daughters most evenings. 'We like to hear what the girls are doing in school,' Michelle Obama once said on television, highlighting the importance of nurturing family ties.

Politics cannot be a lonely path so remember to keep your family close.

4. **Develop a thick skin**: The people who surround you in politics can be very rude. There are instances where politicians are booed in public and have ink thrown on their faces. In mainstream culture, the politician is thought to be an unethical person with nefarious intent. There is some degree of truth to this perception. But aspiring politicians will have to suffer the brunt of these negative impressions by developing a thick skin.

It is likely you will fall victim to crass commentary in your career. You cannot let that get to you. Remember the higher purpose. It is only if you do that you will be able to survive this brutal field.

The three mantras above should help you through tough times. You have to be prepared to take on the toughest challenges and remember that you are working for the public good.

Reflecting on Your Present State

Can you persevere? Do you think you will be able to battle the challenges that politics will throw at you? What makes you think you can? If you are lacking in skills, are you willing to improve on them? Below is a table you should attempt to complete in all earnestness as you prepare yourself for politics.

Are you prepared to	Answer (Yes/No)	Solutions as examples for self-improvement
Take a fair share of criticism from people (even if you are in the right)?		Put yourself further in the public eye to get used to feedback.
Feel comfortable around uber-competitive party workers vying for similar positions?		Learn to study people so you know who you can trust.
Deal with insecurity about your political future?		Meditate to be calm of mind.
Be a problem-solver to all constituents who approach you?		Build networks and connections so you can help others.

Chapter 8

What Is It Like to Be a Woman in Politics?

Only 11 per cent of the parliament in India at present is composed of women. Even fewer women are seen in party leadership positions. We have an unquestionable deficit of women leaders and our society is worse off for it. There are reasons that few women make it to leadership positions. Politics as a profession does not offer a stable work and life balance, and as a male dominated profession, makes it harder for women emotionally. A poor political culture even physically threatens women. We need to bring more women in to political life. If you are a woman who feels passionate about entering the political sphere, I would urge you to prepare yourself with greater vigour than your male counterparts. You need to be able to:

- Understand the issues that women face in politics.
- Start working on solutions to overcome these problems.
- Ready yourself emotionally for the political journey

Reading this chapter will not be enough. Your 'To do' should include:
- Speaking to your family members and loved ones of your political aspirations.

- Actively looking for a mentor who can support you through your political career.
- Planning and preparing for potential issues meticulously.

Looking back...

On 25 June 1908, a nationalist serving as a government doctor and a determined homemaker welcomed a baby girl, Sucheta, to their lives. This was a Bengali family of socially progressive Brahmo Samajis working in Punjab. They expected their daughter to thrive in the career of her choosing. When she decided to study constitutional law at the prestigious Indraprastha College and St Stephen's College, they were very excited. Sucheta went on to teach at the Banaras Hindu University as a lecturer. She was an academic but her passion extended beyond the classroom.

Sucheta Mazumdar joined the Indian independence movement and worked alongside Mahatma Gandhi. Her family supported her decision to be part of such a noble cause. They stood by her decision to fight for India's freedom. During her days as a nationalist, she met with Acharya Kirplani, a prominent leader and freedom fighter. They shared a common interest for the future of India. Perhaps it was their shared vision that made them fall in love. They decided to marry.

Mazumdar travelled extensively with Congress party members as part of the independence movement to which she was committed. She even travelled alone on occasion. She was a terrific organizer and was asked for support on multiple fronts. Her husband was supportive of her work in the party.

Mazumdar built a strong rapport with other Congress

members and was eventually put in charge of building the Mahila Congress Cell. But what Sucheta Mazumdar is most famous for is being the first woman chief minister of Uttar Pradesh, elected to office on 2 October 1963. At a time when men dominated politics even more than they do today, she broke the mould to become a leader.

Sucheta Mazumdar not only had the extensive support of her family and husband, but also the mental strength to be surrounded by men and hold her own.

It is incredibly hard to be a woman in politics. On most occasions, as a woman you might find yourself to be the only woman in a room or on a stage full of men. India's strong patriarchal culture has made it emotionally, physically and logistically difficult for women to enter and grow in the political sphere. When Mulayam Singh Yadav and Azam Khan, prominent leaders from Uttar Pradesh, make public comments about 'boys being boys' to justify rape culture or 'women asking for it' to blame rape victims, most women listening are taken aback. We wonder what is in store for women who work with men like this. It makes us weary about women entering politics.

But we need more women in politics precisely for this reason. We need to have more women leaders so that we can normalize women in public places, and shift the discourse to be more progressive, breaking the glass ceiling of public life. We need women without any political lineage to emerge. But if you are considering a career in politics as a woman, you need to prepare yourself to tackle problems that are likely to emerge.

In this section you will read about the problems that women face in politics.

Problems women face

'There is no particular issue faced by women that would make me say that we have a harder time in politics,' lied a senior Congress leader. I could read from her eyes that she was hesitant about sharing her true views. Most women leaders do not want to show that they are weak and are unwilling to share details of the obstacles they have faced. Systemic and cultural reasons have kept women away from politics. But spending time around women leaders, it is evident that they face greater hardships than men in politics. A woman's character is the first thing attacked. 'She probably had "relations" with the senior party leader,' is a frequent comment that will circulate about women politicians in political parties. Those who rise up the political ladder quickly are suspected to have used their sexuality instead of their talent.

Consider how we are so gender biased against Mayawati or J. Jayalalitha who had terrific political acumen but are still looked at through the lens of their relationships. When we speak of them, we still bring up Kanshi Ram and MGR, respectively. We highlight the men they had relationships with to talk of their political career. There should be no doubt in our minds that these women had the potential and talent to come up independently and that the men in their lives were secondary to this fact. 'After his [MGR's] death, I was left to fend for myself. He didn't create a smoother way for me to become his successor. Though he introduced me to politics, he didn't make anything easy for me. I had to fight and struggle my way up,' Jayalalitha had complained after years of harassment.

We don't trust that powerful women in politics can rise of their own merit.

'I was rising up in the party very quickly. I had been

promoted to the rank of a spokesperson within a year of my joining the party. I knew politics like the back of my hand. After all, I had been a youth leader in my college days and was willing to go in to defend the party on national channels. But instead of appreciating my quick rise, party members passed judgment on me. They said I had "slept my way to the top,"' a senior politician shared with me. Her face turned pale as she narrated the perils of being a woman in politics.

'I went to my husband and told him about the horrible rumours. He told me that people were going to try to shake me and that I had to believe in myself. This was just the beginning,' she told me, with a smile. 'The more I rose up in politics, the nastier the rumours were to get. People disregarded the fact that I was a qualified professional with the capacity to lead. They kept boxing my abilities to my gender,' she continued. Though she smiled, you could see the pain in her eyes. She had gone on to become a minister for a while, but she was still angry about the discrimination she had to face.

A woman in politics has her relationship status and family details become public information. Gossip about her relationship status increases as she rises up the political ladder. If a man has to have a thick skin in politics, then a woman needs to develop an even thicker skin. Marriages are affected as rumours that fly about women politicians. You and your spouse have to have faith and trust in each other through this journey.

- **Skewed work-life balance**: Ideally, household chores should be equally distributed between partners. Unfortunately, in India, women overwhelmingly continue to be responsible for the household. A woman is also expected to be the primary care-giver for the child, responsible by default for all duties to do with children. Though progressive concepts of stay-at-home-dads are more prominent and some fathers do take on more active roles as caretakers, this is just not a widely implemented trend.

Women continue to be the go-to point for all matters relating to the home. This makes it harder for women to pursue political professions which take up a significant amount of time and does not have strict working hours. A woman will be expected to stay away from the home and the children on many occasions. She will be expected to attend late night meetings and might not always be available to the children. Politics takes a toll on one's personal life.

I met with Dr Najma Heptullah, a member of the Rajya Sabha, the deputy speaker of the House, and her husband in their own house. I was in her ornately decorated living room, which had pictures of her three talented and beautiful young daughters. One a doctor, the second a banker and the third a freelancer. They had invited a number of political leaders and were having a small dinner event. Their hospitality was impeccable. Dr Heptullah and her husband bustled across the room to ensure that all guests were well-fed and having a good evening. While Dr Heptullah was checking on the welfare of the guests, her husband was running in and out of the kitchen ensuring that abundant supply of food was available to all. All guests seemed happy.

As we left that evening, I noticed Dr Heptullah handing out small trays of gifts to everyone. I inquired what it was. 'My husband makes it a point to remember what people like to eat. He then has our chef prepare it so that when our guests leave, we are able to provide small favours that they can take home. He has always been thoughtful like that. In fact, as long as I have known him, he has made sure that my friends and colleagues are always well-fed and happy with us,' she said with a smile. The story was telling not just of the supportive marriage that I had witnessed that evening, but also how a committed husband could help his wife do well in politics.

Sheryl Sandberg, the female CEO of Facebook, famously declared that one of the most important decisions that a woman can take is choosing the man she marries. If you are considering marriage, think about your partner and the need for him to be very supportive. If you are married, then have an honest conversation about duties and responsibilities before entering politics. You will need a supportive spouse and family members who will understand the demands of your profession and help you with household tasks and chores. There is the precedent of women politicians who have been able to juggle family, work and politics. You will have to plan for it.

- **The Issue of Physical Safety**: It would be naïve to assume that public life provides for any additional protection for a woman. In fact, politics is a particularly vulnerable profession for women. You are expected to travel to unknown locations by yourself, stay in government guesthouses that might be unsafe, work late into the night with senior party members and are often surrounded by men. There are several stories of women who have, in these conditions, been physically abused by men.

Think about the iconic image of Jayalalitha having

her saree pulled and torn in the Legislative Assembly when she spoke ill of Karunanidhi. Or of Mamata Banerjee being dragged out by her hair from the Writer's Building. Or more recently, the YouTube video of a party worker repeatedly harassing Nagma, that went viral on social media. Unfortunately, the issue of physical safety is not a new topic for most women. But the gaping hole in politics is that there are no channels to complain against those who are harassing women. Political parties don't have an ombudsman programme or a general cell against sexual harassment. In a male dominated space, you are expected to hold your own and deal with problems in your own way. Most women are concerned that if they show fear, they will be called weak and will not be given important positions of power.

It is not unsurprising that in this context, most women workers prefer working in the women's cell or having women companions on the road. The opportunity to work with other women allows you the opportunity to meet other mentors and friends. One cannot undermine the relevance of a strong mentor. As you will see, mentors can be transformational to a woman's career.

How a Woman Survives in Politics

Despite so many perils in a political career, India is fortunate to have had strong women who have led the way for other women leaders to follow. We can brag about having had elected women chief ministers and a woman prime minister. That is much more than most countries can say. If we want to continue to be a country of strong leaders, we need to see what our leaders before us did right and emulate them. Here are some of the things you should keep in mind.

Be invincible. Stay dogged. An individual's mettle is constantly judged in political life. People want to gauge whether you are emotionally strong enough to lead. Women are pushed even harder. Most party workers follow a consistent pattern in judging the strength of a woman, initially mocking and patronizing them in an effort to demoralize them. This often works. Women politicians that stay on and continue to grow within the political sphere take on endless rumours and have their patience endlessly tested. You must be invincible and committed to your cause.

Recognize and accept that more will be asked of you than of your male colleagues. But remember the strength of your decision to stay within the party and lead as a woman. Push back against every rumour and stay true to your cause. This will open up doors for generations of women to come. Your cause is bigger and it is important for you to keep your head in the game.

'I remember I had gone to meet with Rajiv Gandhiji with the strategy of how to win key states. I was waiting in the guest room when I saw him,' a senior woman politician narrated. 'A local party member walked in to the room and signalled for me to come out. He was known to create problems and had in the past mocked me on several occasions. I didn't want to follow him out but didn't want to disrespect him either. So I decided that I would hear him out.

'We stepped out to the lawn outside, and the party worker told me, "Madam, others have been spreading all kinds of rumours about you. I didn't even want to bring it to your attention but I thought you should know. They are saying such despicable things that I can't even repeat them. But please know that they are bad and you need to protect your dignity." I was a bit confused why he had come to me. Then an overwhelming curiosity got to me and I really wanted to know what was being said about me.

'I then remembered something my husband always tells me: when taking in any information, consider if it is useful to you. If it isn't, then don't bother with it. So, I had two options. Either I could ask him about the rumours and run the risk of rattling my nerves before a meeting where I could be given more party responsibility. Or I could walk back in to the waiting room. Keeping my focus about all the matters I wanted to discuss, I let go of what I had just heard. I decided I did not need to know what the party worker had to say. How could it really help me? I kept my focus. I met with Rajivji who asked me to lead the election in a few battleground states. And came home content,' she finished.

She was phenomenal in her capacity to stay focused and remained committed to her calling. She later told me that it gets better for women the longer they stay in politics, because women get used to the rumours. You have to have the same quality. You need to believe yourself to be invincible and stay dogged.

Keep your family close. Strengthen relationships. A significant portion of the last chapter was dedicated to the importance of keeping your family close. This is even more relevant for women. If you are married, then it is pivotal that you prepare your husband to take on more household chores. If you are single, you should set right your parents and relatives' expectations about your upcoming career.

In February 2017, I was in Maharashtra with Vandana Chavan, a Rajya Sabha member from the Nationalist Congress Party, during the municipal elections in Pune. Given her strong brand in the city of having been a pro-development mayor bringing significant progress, she was requested by her party to lead the municipal elections. She was well-respected by her colleagues and held the attention of the room in any situation.

In the two months leading up to the election, the fifty-five-year-old lawyer and mother of two accomplished daughters would leave the house at 8 a.m. and come back at 3 a.m. the next morning. 'Most days, I forget if I have eaten anything,' she says. 'But my mother was nice enough to always send some food over in case I had nothing to eat. She would call me from time to time to check on me. If I am close to her house, I pop in and she makes me lunch or dinner. Sometimes I have gone in as late as ten or eleven at night but she has been nice enough to make me a meal,' she told me. 'On the work front, my husband is also a lawyer and he makes sure that all the cases I have are proceeding well. He files the paper work. And without being asked he does so much for me,' she completed. In those brief few days, it was evident that Vandana had the support of her family. She had been one of the youngest mayors of Pune and is a leader within the NCP.

It is almost impossible for a woman leader to survive without the support network of her family and friends. You will have to rely on those close to you extensively.

Find a mentor. Create a support network. Most women in politics are likely to follow some sort of lineage. A father or a husband who has left behind a vacant seat, or an uncle who is looking for someone to take over the constituency are few of the links that lead women into politics. This family connection allows women the mentorship and support network that they need for political growth. These women are taken under the wing of established politicians who show them the ropes and help them build trust and credibility with party workers.

For those who do not have this support network, it is important to build them. Reach out to other women leaders and look for their mentorship. Having a mentor, especially a woman, can be a very powerful tool for a young woman politician.

A few years ago, I met with a young woman who had recently been elected to the Legislative Assembly. 'I didn't understand politics because I don't come from a political family. I would run odd errands and help the party whenever I could without a concrete direction of where I was headed. This changed when I met with Didi [Mamata Banerjee]. She explained to me the details of the functioning of politics. She told me how to win an election and become valuable to the party. She took me under her wing and guided me. Finally, she gave me a ticket and today I am a member of the Legislative Assembly because of her,' she told me.

Your mentor need not be a chief minister. Women are empathetic to other women colleagues and are often willing to take junior leaders under their wing. Be fierce in reaching out and seeking their support. When you have someone experienced looking out for you, you are twice as likely to succeed.

The solutions section above should give women politicians a strong direction of how they should prepare themselves for politics. You have to customize each of these solutions to your requirements and march forward! Be fierce and be powerful.

Reflecting on Your Present State

There is no second thought to the fact that we need more women in politics. But as you consider your entry in to the political sphere, introspect. Take a piece of paper and respond to these eight questions with three reasons:

Do you know why you are getting into politics?	
Do you feel very strongly about your reason for getting into politics?	
What is the driving force pushing you into politics?	
Are you mentally prepared for the toll that politics will take on your social and personal life (especially your reputation)?	
Do you have the support of your family and/or friends as you pursue this path?	
Have you talked to your husband, family members and other relevant people?	
Have you actively sought out a mentor or supporter to help you guide through politics?	
Have you made an effort to reach out to people and network to find a leader?	

Chapter 9

Closing Thoughts

Politics is not an easy profession. It is, however, a noble profession that can have tremendous impact on the lives of people. In our history classes we learn about famous politicians who introduced policies and programmes that have transformed the course of humanity. Mahatma Gandhi's non-violence movement, Lal Bahadur Shastri's agricultural movement, Rajiv Gandhi's decision to overlook the Shah Bano case and Atal Bihari Vajpayee's aggressive infrastructure expansion are few examples that we know that have changed the way we lead our lives.

There is a lack of definition around the role of a parliamentarian and politician. An unstructured system within the party does not guide the direction you should take. There is no clear understanding about what will help you prepare professionally for a life in politics. There are innumerable issues around your ability to support yourself financially through your political career. Politics certainly takes a toll on your personal and family life. This book has highlighted each of these problems with potential solutions to help you prepare yourself. But political journeys are so unpredictable that it is virtually impossible to be fully prepared for each and every turn. But it is a chance worth taking, despite the suffering and panic.

Reflecting on Your Present State

There is no second thought to the fact that we need more women in politics. But as you consider your entry in to the political sphere, introspect. Take a piece of paper and respond to these eight questions with three reasons:

Do you know why you are getting into politics?	
Do you feel very strongly about your reason for getting into politics?	
What is the driving force pushing you into politics?	
Are you mentally prepared for the toll that politics will take on your social and personal life (especially your reputation)?	
Do you have the support of your family and/or friends as you pursue this path?	
Have you talked to your husband, family members and other relevant people?	
Have you actively sought out a mentor or supporter to help you guide through politics?	
Have you made an effort to reach out to people and network to find a leader?	

Chapter 9

Closing Thoughts

Politics is not an easy profession. It is, however, a noble profession that can have tremendous impact on the lives of people. In our history classes we learn about famous politicians who introduced policies and programmes that have transformed the course of humanity. Mahatma Gandhi's non-violence movement, Lal Bahadur Shastri's agricultural movement, Rajiv Gandhi's decision to overlook the Shah Bano case and Atal Bihari Vajpayee's aggressive infrastructure expansion are few examples that we know that have changed the way we lead our lives.

There is a lack of definition around the role of a parliamentarian and politician. An unstructured system within the party does not guide the direction you should take. There is no clear understanding about what will help you prepare professionally for a life in politics. There are innumerable issues around your ability to support yourself financially through your political career. Politics certainly takes a toll on your personal and family life. This book has highlighted each of these problems with potential solutions to help you prepare yourself. But political journeys are so unpredictable that it is virtually impossible to be fully prepared for each and every turn. But it is a chance worth taking, despite the suffering and panic.

CLOSING THOUGHTS

I have heard a great deal of the perils of a political life from many politicians. But I have also heard of the rewards of leadership. The content faces of those to whom you bring positive impact can be powerful. They tell me it is worth those sleepless nights, maddening travels and emotional tribulations.

A wise man once told me a practice he takes on whenever he feels overwhelmed with politics. 'Close your eyes. Take a deep breath. Clear your mind. Think of the person who you truly look up to. Don't dwell too much on it but just note down names that you feel are the most promising leaders you have known. I can promise you that you will think of at least one political leader. Ask yourself whether you want to be like that leader. If the answer is yes, then you are ready to fight on.'

Be ready to fight because it will seem like a long one.

'Two things happen under extreme pressure: matter is crushed and diamonds are formed.'

– Nike, circa 2000